NEW DIRECTIONS FOR HIGHER EDUCATION

Martin Kramer, *University of California, Berkeley*
EDITOR-IN-CHIEF

Faculty in Governance: The Role of Senates and Joint Committees in Academic Decision Making

Robert Birnbaum
University of Maryland, College Park

EDITOR

CENTER FOR HIGHER EDUCATION GOVERNANCE AND LEADERSHIP
4114 CSS Building, University of Maryland, College Park, Maryland 20742-2435   (301) 405-5582

Number 75, Fall 1991

JOSSEY-BASS INC., PUBLISHERS, San Francisco
MAXWELL MACMILLAN INTERNATIONAL PUBLISHING GROUP
New York • Oxford • Singapore • Sydney • Toronto

CENTER FOR HIGHER EDUCATION GOVERNANCE AND LEADERSHIP

4114 CSS Building, University of Maryland, College Park, Maryland 20742-2435   (301) 405-5582

FACULTY IN GOVERNANCE: THE ROLE OF SENATES AND JOINT COMMITTEES
IN ACADEMIC DECISION MAKING
Robert Birnbaum (ed.)
New Directions for Higher Education, no. 75
Volume XIX, number 3
Martin Kramer, Editor-in-Chief

Microfilm copies of issues and articles are available in 16mm and 35mm,
as well as microfiche in 105mm, through University Microfilms Inc., 300
North Zeeb Road, Ann Arbor, Michigan 48106.

LC 85-644752   ISSN 0271-0560   ISBN 1-55542-771-5

NEW DIRECTIONS FOR HIGHER EDUCATION is part of The Jossey-Bass
Higher and Adult Education Series and is published quarterly by Jossey-
Bass Inc., Publishers, 350 Sansome Street, San Francisco, California 94104-
1310 (publication number USPS 990-880). Second-class postage paid at
San Francisco, California, and at additional mailing offices. POSTMASTER:
Send address changes to New Directions for Higher Education, Jossey-
Bass Inc., Publishers, 350 Sansome Street, San Francisco, California 94104-
1310.

SUBSCRIPTIONS for 1991 cost $45.00 for individuals and $60.00 for institutions, agencies, and libraries.

EDITORIAL CORRESPONDENCE should be sent to the Editor-in-Chief,
Martin Kramer, 2807 Shasta Road, Berkeley, California 94708.

Cover photograph and random dot by Richard Blair/Color & Light © 1990.

Printed on acid-free paper in the United States of America.

CONTENTS

EDITOR'S NOTES   1
Robert Birnbaum

1. The Latent Organizational Functions of the Academic Senate: 7
Why Senates Do Not Work but Will Not Go Away
Robert Birnbaum
Senates may not do what they are supposed to do, but they are nevertheless
important to higher education.

2. Participative Governance Bodies in Higher Education: 27
Report of a National Study
Joseph E. Gilmour, Jr.
Campus leaders at over 90 percent of institutions responding to a 1989
survey indicated that they had a senate or other participative governance
body and that they were generally pleased with its performance.

3. Campus Leaders and Campus Senates   41
Barbara A. Lee
Senates are more likely to be effective if certain principles are followed by
both faculty and administrative leaders.

4. Faculty Involvement in Institutional Budgeting   63
John G. Dimond
"Shared authority" suggests that faculty should participate in making institutional financial decisions, but this does not happen extensively at research universities.

5. Joint Big Decision Committees and University Governance   79
Myrtle M. Yamada
Joint Big Decision Committees have been proposed as a preferred new
form of academic governance. Do they really work as their advocates say
they do?

INDEX   97

EDITOR'S NOTES

During the late 1960s and early 1970s, the role of faculty and academic senates in governance was a burning issue for many American colleges and universities. Institutions of higher education were caught in the whirlwind of international and domestic crises, and on campus, as in the body politic at large, neither old answers nor old forums were considered legitimate merely because they had traditionally been accepted in the past.

Finding answers to the questions Who decides? and Who decides who decides? were no longer academic exercises but real-life dramas that often determined whether an institution functioned or closed down, whether an administration survived or fell, and whether faculty fulfilled their traditional activities or participated in guerrilla warfare against "the establishment." Yeats's prophetic vision—"Things fall apart, the center cannot hold; mere anarchy is loosed upon the world"—had come to pass even in our once idyllic groves. The public considered campus unrest the nation's most critical problem, and scholars of higher education made the study of academic governance a major concern.

Then, suddenly, interest in governance came to a halt. In the decade between 1975 and 1985, the subject was no longer a major item on the higher education agenda. This dramatic decline in interest was probably less an indication that the questions had been satisfactorily resolved than an indication that other problems had become more pressing in the inexorable flow of institutional life. Institutions that had been braced for projected enrollment and fiscal declines that never came felt less stressed, and the relative availability of resources made it possible to divide the wealth with relatively little attention paid to the processes through which those resources were allocated.

Now in 1990, governance issues are once more becoming a focus of attention in higher education. Faculties, administrators, and trustees are again beginning to examine their roles in academic decision making and question the structures and processes through which they interact and influence each other. Part of this new interest may be due merely to the cyclical nature of institutional issues and to an endemic tension between faculty and administration that ensures that periodically at least one of the major governance constituencies will articulate dissatisfaction with existing structures or processes. Recent reports reflect that tension and suggest that faculty continue to be dissatisfied with their administrations. For example, only 57 percent of a national sample of full-time faculty were recently reported as satisfied with the quality of their chief administrative officers, and only 54 percent with the relationship between administration and faculty on their campus (Russell and others, 1990). Similarly, 60 percent of the faculty respondents in a 1984 national survey identified their campuses as autocratic, and 64 percent believed the administration to be only "fair" or "poor" (Boyer, 1987). A comparable study conducted five years later indicated that only 50 percent of the faculty respondents believed that their institutions were being effectively managed (Carnegie Foundation for the Advancement of Teaching, 1989). Perhaps nothing has really changed in the 70 years since Veblen ([1918] 1957), the consummate faculty member, castigated deans and presidents and argued that an effective university could exist only when their roles were abolished so that faculty could manage their own affairs.

The resurgence of interest in governance may also be due in part to the concerns for declining resources in the face of (again) predicted enrollment downturns (when resources decline, interest in participating in allocation decisions becomes more contentious) or to the increased involvement of state offices in institutional affairs. Faculty realize that their ability to exert influence is weakened as institutions become more subject to external mandates for academic accountability, and find mid-year budget recisions a constant fact of life. Problems of campus instability may become even more pressing in the future as large numbers of faculty retire, only to be replaced by neophytes who lack experience with, and understanding of, traditional governance processes. Just such a massive influx of new faculty in the 1960s may have contributed to the significant disruption of governance patterns at that time.

The work of scholars in the period roughly between the mid 1960s and 1970s provided valuable data and wisdom that assisted institutions to assess, improve, or replace their own governance systems. Much of this material can be profitably read today. At the same time, it is time to look at new governance realities and to consider different paradigms for thinking about how institutional structures and interactions can be studied. This work has already been started by many of our colleagues whose ideas are cited throughout this volume. We hope that this volume contributes to this process.

Just as institutions can be considered systems, composed of smaller subsystems and existing as components of even larger systems (Birnbaum, 1988), so campus governance issues can be considered at various levels. The highest level contemplates the relationship of colleges and universities to the social, economic, and political systems of which they are a part. The lowest level considers ways in which campus subunits, such as colleges, departments, or research institutes, are structured and operated. In this volume, we consider governance at an intermediate level by examining the institution as a whole and focusing particularly on the means by which faculty find collective voice through representative bodies, such as academic senates. The authors approach the topic using a wide range of perspectives and methodologies.

In the first chapter, Robert Birnbaum summarizes the criticisms that have been leveled against academic senates and explains why academic senates may be important to colleges and universities even though they don't fulfill the functions for which they were ostensibly created. Arguing that the senate's effectiveness depends on the model of organization through which it is considered, he suggests that while senates may not appear to be working according to managerial, collegial, or political views, they may have important symbolic functions that make them an indispensable component of an organized anarchy. Birnbaum takes an affectionate view of the senate, but one unlikely to find favor in the eyes of those who advocate its importance as an instrumental agency for shared governance.

Those wishing to argue against Birnbaum's perspective can find some support for their position in Chapter Two in Joseph E. Gilmour, Jr.'s recent survey of senates and other participative governance bodies. Gilmour finds not only that senates are essentially ubiquitous in higher education but that campus respondents agree in general that these bodies deal with important institutional issues, that they operate efficiently, and that they fulfill important governance roles. In addition to presenting evidence about senate functions, Gilmour fills a significant gap in our knowledge of academic organization by presenting the only current data available on senate structure and membership. Gilmour notes the discrepancy between his views of the senate and those of Birnbaum and acknowledges that those responding to his survey (presidents and senate chairs) may have biased judgments because of their vested interest in believing the senates to be successful.

Barbara A. Lee's analysis of the effectiveness of senates, based on case studies constructed from intensive interviews with campus-based governance participants, is less sanguine than Gilmour's data might suggest. Examining the dynamics of governance in real settings provides a richness of data not possible using a survey methodology, and in Chapter Three Lee describes how senates work—or don't work—in three different institutions. In one, the governance system is described by its participants as effective; the other two are characterized as either "troubled" or "paralyzed." The critical factors, according to Lee, are structure, culture, and administrative attitudes toward governance. Although administrative leadership, in particular, can make a critical difference, some situations are essentially beyond the control of campus leaders.

While the first three chapters look at the general role of senates in institutions of all kinds, the next two focus on research universities and the ways in which faculty and administrators influence institutional policy through committees. In Chapter Four, John G. Dimond examines the faculty role in budgeting. He uses the Research I and II institutions in Gilmour's study as his sample, but supplements Gilmour's survey data with telephone interviews of faculty leaders. Dimond finds that faculty on most campuses have some degree of involvement with budgets, either through senates or membership in administrative committees, but that only in a small number of instances do they exercise the kind of detailed and comprehensive participation that might be thought of as reflecting "joint effort." Faculty participation as it now exists in many institutions may be more shadow than substance.

Myrtle M. Yamada is also interested in faculty influence, but the focus of her attention in Chapter Five is on a "new" governance structure called the Joint Big Decision Committee (JBDC), which engages both faculty and administrative members in the development of institutional academic and fiscal strategy. The JBDC was originally studied and advocated by George Keller (Keller, 1983) as an important way to improve the management of colleges and universities. Yamada revisited many of the institutions described by Keller to assess the effectiveness of their JBDC. She finds that these structures have had no effect on academic affairs, but under certain circumstances can enhance faculty involvement in financial priorities and improve the quality of decision making. Unfortunately, she points out, claims that the use of JBDCs is increasing do not appear to be accurate.

Taken collectively, these chapters provide an indeterminate answer to the question of whether senates and similar governance structures are effective. All five chapters agree on at least three things. First, whatever their other merits, senates and other governance bodies serve important symbolic functions at academic institutions. Second, at least in some institutions some of the time, they serve important instrumental functions as well. And third, faculty satisfaction with their governance roles is not always correlated with their actual level of influence. On some campuses, faculty can be displeased with their lack of influence over policy. But at others, faculty appear quite content with playing a passive role. If there is any lesson here, it may be that the only "best" form of campus governance structure is the one found to be satisfactory by the participants.

Dissatisfaction with existing governance systems, where it exists, can provide colleges and universities with a healthy incentive for institutional improvement. If handled well by institutional leaders, governance changes can lead to self-renewal. If handled poorly, particularly under conditions of stress or crisis, changes can lead to institutional disruption.

If issues of senates and governance are to continue on the higher education agenda for at least the near future, there are at least three things that can be done to make the discussion more enlightened and fruitful. First, research might be initiated that would provide the academic community with basic descriptive data about the present state of governance at all three levels (system, institution, and subunit). The Gilmour and Dimond studies provide a first (but limited) step. Institutional leaders reconsidering their governance processes have no structured way to compare characteristics of their governance system to those of other institutions, learn of alternative structures and processes, or become familiar with innovative or exemplary processes elsewhere. Development of a national data base would permit institutions to compare their systems with those of others of similar size, program, or control. The governance system of every institution is— and should be—different from that of every other, because their histories, cultures, and relationships are different. The purpose of a national data bank would not be to make governance systems more alike, but to help institutions ground their discussion in reality.

Second, a formal, structured process of institutional self-examination could be developed that can help trustees, administrators, and faculty leaders assess the quality and effectiveness of governance on their own campus, make informed judgments about what is working and what is not, and offer procedural suggestions for collective self-improvement. Such a process should be initiated on a campus *before* governance problems become uncontrollable. Preventing governance systems from becoming dysfunctional may not be easy, but correcting them once they are paralyzed may be impossible. Some or all of the factors identified by Lee as influencing the effectiveness of a senate might provide a starting place for such a review.

And third, one or more national organizations could initiate a new dialogue on the meaning of shared authority and joint effort. It is almost a quarter of a century since the development of the last such widely supported normative statement. As we enter the 1990s, perhaps it is time to publicly reconfirm a continued commitment to the ideals contained in the joint "Statement of Government of Colleges and Universities" or else to consider a new statement that more accurately reflects either what academic governance is or what it should be.

Robert Birnbaum
Editor

References

Birnbaum, R. *How Colleges Work: The Cybernetics of Academic Organization and Leadership.* San Francisco: Jossey-Bass, 1988.

Boyer, E. L. *College: The Undergraduate Experience in America.* New York: Harper & Row, 1987.

Carnegie Foundation for the Advancement of Teaching. *The Condition of the Professoriate: Attitudes and Trends, 1989.* Princeton, N.J.: Princeton University Press, 1989.

Keller, G. *Academic Strategy: The Management Revolution in American Higher Education.* Baltimore, Md.: Johns Hopkins University Press, 1983.

Russell, S. H., Cox, R. S., Williamson, C., Boismier, J., Javitz, H., Fairweather, J., and Zimbler, L. J. *Faculty in Higher Education Institutions, 1988: Contractor Report.* Washington, D.C.: National Center for Educational Statistics, 1990.

Veblen, T. *The Higher Learning in America.* New York: Sagamore Press, 1957. (Originally published 1918.)

Robert Birnbaum is professor of higher education at the University of Maryland, College Park. His most recent book is How Colleges Work: The Cybernetics of Academic Organization and Leadership *(1988).*

*Academic senates are criticized as ineffective, yet they remain a
central component of governance on most campuses. Why do
senates persist if they don't appear to work?*

The Latent Organizational Functions of the Academic Senate: Why Senates Do Not Work but Will Not Go Away

Robert Birnbaum

The term *academic senate* is used in this chapter to identify a formal,
representative governance structure at the institutional level that may
include only faculty (a "pure" senate) or that, in addition to a faculty
majority, may also include representatives of other campus constituencies,
such as administrators, academic staff members, and/or students (a "mixed"
senate), as defined by the Report of the American Association for Higher
Education Task Force on Faculty Representation and Academic Negotia-
tions (American Association for Higher Education, 1967, p. 34).

Academic senates generally are considered the normative organizational structure through which faculty exercise their role in college and
university governance at the institutional level (American Association for
Higher Education, 1967). Although no complete census is available, analyses
of data in past studies (Kemerer and Baldridge, 1975; Hodgkinson, 1974)
suggest that senates may exist in one form or another on 60 to 80 percent
of all campuses.

With the advent of faculty collective bargaining in the late 1960s, con-

This chapter was prepared pursuant to a grant from the Office of Educational
Research and Improvement/Department of Education (OERI/ED). However, the
opinions expressed herein do not necessarily reflect the position or policy of
OERI/ED, and no official endorsement by OERI/ED should be inferred. This chapter first appeared in the *Journal of Higher Education*, 1989, 60 (4), 423–442, and is
reprinted by permission.

cern was expressed that senates, unable to compete with the more adversarial and aggressive union, might disappear on many campuses (McConnell and Mortimer, 1971). Not only has this prediction proved false (Baldridge, Kemerer, and Associates, 1981; Begin, 1979), but there is evidence that the number of institutions with senates has increased over the past decades (Baldridge and others, 1978).

This growth is somewhat perplexing in view of the criticisms that have increasingly been directed against the senate structure. It has been called weak, ineffective, an empty forum, vestigial, unrepresentative, and inept (Baldridge, 1982; Carnegie Foundation for the Advancement of Teaching, 1983; Keller, 1983; Mason, 1972; Millett, 1978; McConnell and Mortimer, 1971). Its detractors have referred to it as "slowly collapsing and becoming dormant" (Keller, 1983, p. 61) and "purely ceremonial" (Ben-David, 1972, p. 19). In a 1969 national study, 60 percent of faculty respondents rated the performance of their campus senate or faculty council as only "fair" or "poor" (Carnegie Commission on Higher Education, 1973). A more recent consideration of faculty governance has stated that "traditional structures do not appear to be working very well. Faculty participation has declined, and we discovered a curious mismatch between the agenda of faculty councils and the crisis now confronted by many institutions" (Carnegie Foundation for the Advancement of Teaching, 1983, p. 12).

These negative evaluations of faculty governance structures are not new. A trenchant observer in 1918 (Veblen, [1918] 1957, p. 186) noted the administrative use of faculty "committees-for-the-sifting-of-the-sawdust" to give the appearance, but not the reality, of participation, and called them "a nice problem in self-deception, chiefly notable for an endless proliferation" (p. 206).

There is not complete agreement that the senate has no real instrumental value. Blau's (1973, p. 164) finding of a negative correlation between senate participation and educational centralization at over 100 colleges and universities, for example, led him to state that "an institutionalized faculty government is not mere window dressing but an effective mechanism for restricting centralized control over educational programs, in accordance with the professional demands of the faculty. Formal institutionalization of faculty authority fortifies it." Another supporter of the senate (Floyd, 1985, p. 26), after reviewing the literature, reported that the senate continued to be "a useful mechanism for campus-wide faculty participation" at certain types of research universities and elite liberal arts colleges in some governance areas, although it was less useful in others. But despite the support of a small number of observers, the clear weight of evidence and authoritative opinion suggests that except perhaps in a small number of institutions with particular characteristics, the academic senate does not work. Indeed, it has been suggested that it has never worked (Baldridge, 1982). Yet it survives and in many respects thrives.

After citing a litany of major criticisms of senates and proposing reasons for deficiencies, Lieberman (1969, p. 65) added, "What is needed is not so much a critique of their inherent weaknesses, but an explanation of their persistence in spite thereof." Similarly, Hobbs (1975), in looking at the functions of university committees, suggested that rather than focusing attention on recommending ways in which these committees might be made more effective, greater attention should be given to examining their roles in university organization. This chapter will conduct such an examination by considering the roles that senates are presumed to play—and the roles they actually play—within four alternative organizational models that consider the senate as part of bureaucratic, collegial, political, or symbolic organizational systems.

Manifest and Latent Functions

The manifest functions of an organizational structure, policy, or practice can be thought of as those for which behavior leads to some specified and related achievement. Institutional processes that usually lead to expected and desired outcomes should be expected to persist. Often, however, organizations engage in behavior that persists over time even though the manifest function is clearly not achieved. Indeed, such behavior may persist even when there is significant evidence that the ostensible function *cannot* be achieved. There is a tendency to label such organizational behavior as irrational or superstitious and to identify an institution's inability to alter such apparently ineffectual behavior as due to "inertia" or "lack of leadership."

Merton's (1957) concept of functional analysis suggests an alternative explanation. Some practices that do not appear to be fulfilling their formally intended functions may persist because they are fulfilling unintended and unrecognized latent functions that are important to the organization. As Merton describes it, functional analysis examines social practices to determine both the planned and intended (manifest) outcomes and the unplanned and unintended (latent) outcomes. This is particularly useful for the study of otherwise puzzling organizational behavior because it "clarifies the analysis of seemingly irrational social patterns, . . . directs attention to theoretically fruitful fields of inquiry, . . . and precludes the substitution of naive moral judgments for sociological analysis" (Merton, 1957, pp. 64–65, 70). In particular, it points toward the close examination of persistent yet apparently ineffective institutional processes or structures to explore the possibility that they are meeting less obvious, but still important, organizational needs. "We should ordinarily (not invariably) expect persistent social patterns and social structures to perform positive functions which are at the time not adequately fulfilled by other existing patterns and structures" (Merton, 1957, p. 72). The senate may do more than many of its critics believe, and "only when we attend to all the functions and their social contexts can we fully appreciate what it is that the senate does" (Tierney, 1983, p. 174).

This chapter will examine two major questions. First, and briefly, what manifest functions of the academic senate do its critics claim not to be fulfilled, and what organizational models do they imply? Second, and at greater depth, what may be the latent functions of the academic senate that may explain its growth and persistence despite its failure to meet its avowed purposes, and how do these functions relate to organizational models?

The Manifest Functions of the Academic Senate

In general, those who criticize the senate have not clearly articulated the criteria they have employed, and their analyses tend to be narrative and anecdotal, with no explicit conceptual orientation. Their comments and conclusions, however, suggest that they evaluate the senate implicitly using the three traditional models of the university as a bureaucracy, a political system, and a collegium.

Probably the most prevalent implicit model is that of the university as bureaucracy. In his study of the effectiveness of senates (which is one of the few studies to specify desired outcomes), Millett (1978, p. xiv) established eight criteria that "would provide some reasonable conclusions about the contributions and the effectiveness of campuswide governance to the process of institutional decision making." These included the extent to which senates clarified institutional purpose, specified program objectives, re-allocated income resources, and developed new income sources, as well as the extent to which they were involved in issues such as the management of operations, degree requirements, academic behavior, and program evaluation. The identification of the senate's role in decision making and the emphasis on goal setting, resource allocation, and evaluation suggest an implicit view of the senate as an integral part of a hierarchical, rational organization. This bureaucratic orientation is also seen in one of the two "modal" university committee types identified by Hobbs (1975). This type, among other characteristics, meets often, has a decision-making function, records minutes, prepares written reports for administrative officers, and has a clear sense of task. Other analysts have also used language that either explicitly or metaphorically identifies the senate in bureaucratic terms. Senates are needed to deal with "the full range of academic and administrative matters" (Carnegie Foundation for the Advancement of Teaching, 1983, p. 13), their purpose "approximates that of the college's management" (Keller, 1983, p. 126), and they assist "the discovery and employment of techniques to deal with deficit spending, with increasing enrollments, with healing the wounds resulting from student dissent, with curriculum expansion, with faculty salary increases in a tight budget, with parking, and so forth" (Stone, 1977, p. 40).

A second model implicitly views the senate as part of a political system. In this model, the senate is seen as a forum for the articulation of interests and as the setting in which decisions on institutional policies and goals are reached through compromise, negotiation, and the formation of coalitions. Senates serve as places for campus politicians to exercise their trade, which at worst may identify them as "poorly attended oratorical bodies" (Keller, 1983, p. 127) and at best means that they can "provide a forum for the resolution of a wide range of issues involving the mission and operation of the institution" (American Association for Higher Education, 1967, p. 57). Given the significant differences that typify the interest groups that make up its constituencies, the senate enables participants to deal with inevitable conflict as they "engage one another civilly in dispute" (Hobbs, 1975, p. 242).

The model of the university as collegium is less explicitly identified in analyses of the senate than the other two models, but it appears to be recognized through constant references in the literature to the concept of collegiality. The senate in this view would be a forum for achieving Millett's (1962) goal of a dynamic of consensus.

Depending on the organizational assumptions used, an observer might consider the senate to be effective in governance (1) to the extent that it efficiently considered institutional problems and, through rational processes, developed rules, regulations, and procedures that resolved them, (2) to the extent that, perceived as fully representative of its constituencies, it formulated and clarified goals and policies, or (3) to the extent that, through interaction in the senate forum, it developed shared values leading to consensus. But senates often appear to do none of these things well. From the bureaucratic perspective, they are slow and inefficient; from a political position, they are oligarchical and not representative; and from a collegial viewpoint, faculty interactions may be as likely to expose latent conflict as to increase feelings of community (Mortimer and McConnell, 1978).

These alternative organizational models suggest a range of activities, processes, and outcomes as the manifest functions of the senate. Because these functions do not appear to be performed adequately, the senate has been judged ineffective. In many ways, the senate appears to be a solution looking for problems. Millett (1978), for example, provides a list of eight specific problems and questions raised by student activism in the 1960s (such as the role of higher education in defense research or the role of higher education in providing community service to the disadvantaged) to which appropriately comprised senates were presumably an answer. He found that "there is very little evidence that organs of campuswide governance, after they were established, were particularly effective in resolving these issues" (p. 200).

The Latent Functions of the Academic Senate

Because its manifest functions are not being fulfilled, the persistence of the senate suggests that it is filling important latent functions. What might some of these be?

The Senate as Symbol. In addition to whatever effects they may have on outcomes, organizational structures and processes often have symbolic importance to participants (Feldman and March, 1981). Academic senates may fill a number of important symbolic functions. We will consider three: the senate as symbolizing institutional membership in the higher education system, the senate as symbolizing collective and individual faculty commitment to professional values, and the senate as symbolizing joint faculty-administration acceptance of existing authority relationships.

Faculty participation in governance generally is accepted as an essential characteristic of "mainstream" colleges and universities. Since 1950, there has been a significant increase in the types and kinds of institutions that many consider only marginally identified with higher education. These include, for example, community colleges with strong administrative hierarchies, unselective state colleges with traditions rooted in teacher education and the paternalistic practices of school systems, and small and unselective independent institutions with authoritarian presidents. By establishing an academic senate structure more typical of the system to which they aspired than it was of the one from which they developed, an institution can suggest the existence of faculty authority even when it does not exist. This structural symbol of a faculty voice can support a claim to being a "real" college.

The development of a senate can also symbolize a general faculty commitment to substantive values. The most visible and public matters of faculty concern at some institutions have been related to faculty collective bargaining, which has tended to focus on employee issues that in many ways are similar to those of other workers. Particularly in the public sector, but sometimes in the private sector as well, faculty emphasis on salary, working conditions, and other mundane matters has eroded, in the minds of the public, their claim to professional status. Creating a senate may be a response to that erosion, symbolizing a commitment to professional values and faculty concern for more purely academic matters. This helps to legitimate the institution's desire to be treated differently from other organizations and also the faculty's claim to be treated differently from other groups of workers. Through a senate, faculty members can symbolically endorse such desirable attributes or outcomes as increased quality, standards, and integrity, even though (or perhaps because) they cannot define either the problems or their solutions in operational terms. The senate may thus serve as a forum through which, individually and collectively, faculty may symbolically embrace values in lieu of actual behavior. Within the senate, academics who have never had controversial new ideas can publicly defend academic freedom, and those without scholarly interests can argue for reduced teaching loads to encourage research. In this way, even faculty who cannot do so through the publication of scholarship or research can publicly display their academic bona fides.

Senates may also serve as symbols of campus authority relationships. A major criticism against the senate is that it exists at the pleasure of the administration and board of trustees (Lieberman, 1969; Baldridge, Curtis, Ecker, and Riley, 1978). Because of this, its authority has been described as "tenuous" (Mortimer and McConnell, 1978, p. 26). However, although trustees have rejected senate recommendations, they have not abolished senates (except in rare circumstances involving the introduction of faculty collective bargaining). Indeed, administrations support senates and believe them to be even more effective than do faculty members (Hodgkinson, 1974). Why should both the faculty and the administration continue to support the senate structure? It is obvious that faculty would wish to maintain senates because they are a symbol of administrative acceptance of the idea of faculty participation in governance. Administrators may support senates because voluntary faculty participation in such bodies is a tacit acknowledgment by faculty members that they recognize and accept the ultimate legal authority of the administration and board. The senate is thus a symbol of cooperation between faculty and administration. As in other organizational settings, parties may cooperate in perpetuating an already established structure even when the objective utility of the structure is agreed by the parties to be of little value (Deutsch, 1973). The continued existence of the senate, therefore, is not only a visible manifestation of the ability of the parties to cooperate but also a reflection of an intent to further increase cooperative activities.

The symbolic value of the senate is so strong that even those like Millett (1978), who have concluded that the senate is ineffective when evaluated against specific criteria, continue to support it. Even if the senate does not work in terms of its ostensible aims, it may be preferable that an institution have a nonfunctioning senate than have no senate at all.

The Senate as Status Provider. Cohen and March (1979, pp. 201–202) have suggested that "most people in a college are most of the time less concerned with the content of a decision than they are with eliciting an acknowledgment of their importance within the community. . . . Faculty members are more insistent on their right to participate in faculty deliberations than they are on exercising that right." In an analogous vein, the existence of a senate certifies the status of faculty members by acknowledging their right to participate in governance, while at the same time not obligating them to do so. The vigorous support of faculty for a strong and active voice in campus governance, coupled with reluctance to give the time that such participation would require (Dykes, 1968; Corson, 1960), should not, therefore, be surprising.

The senate also offers a route of social mobility for older and less prestigious faculty locals whose desire for status based on traditional norms is frustrated by a lack of scholarly achievement (Ladd and Lipset, 1973). Participation in committee affairs, along with the opportunities it brings to work with higher-status administrators, provides a local means for enhancing their own importance.

In addition to certifying the status of participants in general, providing an opportunity for individuals to serve as senators is a means of conferring status that protects the institution from two quite different but potentially disruptive elements: informal leaders and organizational deviants.

Universities are normative organizations that rely on the manipulation of symbols to control the behavior of their members (Etzioni, 1964). Unlike organizations characterized by control through coercive or utilitarian power, normative organizations tend to have more "formal leaders" (those who influence others through their personal power and through the organizational positions they hold) and fewer informal leaders (personal power only) or officials (positional power only). Formal leadership provides a relatively effective means of exercising power in a decentralized and loosely coupled system. By the same token, the development of informal leaders can be dysfunctional if it facilitates the development of semiautonomous subgroups that can diminish the formal leader's influence.

Formal leaders are not able to prevent the development of informal leaders, but in normative organizations "to the degree that informal leaders arise, . . . the tendency is to recruit them and gain their loyalty and cooperation by giving them part-time organizational positions. . . . The tendency is for the informal leaders to lose this status within the given organization and for control to remain largely in the hands of the formal leaders" (Etzioni, 1964, p. 64). Membership in a prestigious body such as a senate with presumed quasi-administrative responsibilities can be used toward the same end "of providing alternative channels of social mobility for those otherwise excluded from the more conventional avenues for 'social advancement' " (Merton, 1957, p. 76). Senate membership provides legitimate organizational roles in which informal leaders can participate and have their status confirmed while at the same time preventing them from disrupting ongoing organizational structures and processes.

There is a second group of campus participants whose activities, if not channeled through a legitimate structure such as a senate, might prove disruptive to the organization. They are the institutional deviants, often highly vocal persons with a single-minded devotion to one or another cause. Senates offer these deviant faculty a legitimized opportunity to vent their grievances and solicit potential support. Election of such persons may sometimes lead administrators to discount the senate as "nonrepresentative" and may be seen by them as yet another example of senate weakness. On the other hand, the need for even deviants to allocate attention means that time spent acting in the relatively stable environment of the senate is time they do not have available for participating in relatively more vulnerable settings, such as the department. The senate may thus serve as a system for absorbing the energies of potentially disruptive faculty members. Because the senate, like the administration, is subject to overload, it can attend to only a small number of items at any one time. The difficulty of convincing senate colleagues of the justice of their position is more likely to reduce aspirations of deviants than would be constant rebuffs by administrators or departmental colleagues; if a faculty member cannot convince his or her colleagues, how can the administration possibly be convinced?

The Senate as Garbage Can and Deep Freeze. Sometimes a college or university can use rational processes to make choices and solve problems when it is called upon to make a decision. However, this becomes difficult when other people become involved in the decision process, new problems are introduced, and new solutions are proposed. These independent streams of participants, problems, and solutions may somehow become attached to each other, often by chance, just as if they were all dumped into a large container, leading to what has been referred to as "garbage can decision making" (Cohen, March, and Olsen, 1972). Choices become more difficult as they become increasingly connected with "garbage" (that is, with problems, potential solutions, or new participants who, at least to the decision maker, appear irrelevant). Choices become easier if they can be made either before these irrelevant matters become attached to them (decision making by oversight), or after these irrelevant matters can be made to leave the choice (decision making by flight). Because of the essential ambiguity of the college and university processes, any choice point can become a garbage can. One of the latent functions of the senate may be to serve as a structural garbage can, and the inability of the senate to make speedy decisions may increase its effectiveness in this role by putting some problems into an organizational "deep freeze."

An administrator who wishes to make a decision but finds it difficult to do so because irrelevant problems have become associated with it can refer those irrelevant problems to the senate. The decision can then be made by flight while the attention of participants is directed elsewhere.

The deliberate speed of the senate makes it possible for many problems that are referred to it to resolve themselves over time with no need for any specific action. This kind of outcome is shown by the disparaging statement of one faculty member that "the committees [of the senate] report, but usually it has taken so long to 'study the issue' that the matter is long since past" (Baldridge, Curtis, Ecker, and Riley, 1978, p. 80).

Other issues, particularly those that deal with goals and values and thus that might be divisive if an attempt were made to resolve them, may be referred to the senate with the justifiable expectation that they will absorb a significant amount of energy and then will not be heard of again. Still, the senate debate has an important outcome even if it does not lead to action. Through the presentation of alternative positions and arguments, participants come to realize that an issue whose resolution initially appeared to be self-evident and therefore enjoying wide support is in fact complex and contentious. As the attractiveness of simplistic solutions is reduced, aspirations are modified and potential conflict is therefore managed.

The Senate as Attention Cue. The number of problems available in a university searching for decision opportunities and forums in which problems can be resolved, although perhaps finite in number, is at any specific time far greater than can be acted on. Administrative attention is in comparatively short supply, and as administrators "look for work," they must decide to which of many different potential attention cues they should pay attention. This is a nontrivial issue because the ability of problems, solutions, decision makers, and choice opportunities to become coupled through temporal rather than logical relationships makes it exceptionally difficult for an administrator to know on an a priori basis what is most important. In the absence of a calculus or algorithm that permits administrators to predict how important any specific problem may prove to be, they must rely on heuristics (such as "oil the squeaky wheel") to indicate when an item may have reached a level of concern sufficient to require administrative attention. There are many sources of such cues—for example, a telephone call from a state legislator or an editorial in the local paper or student press.

Discussion and action (potential or actual) by the senate also serve as an attention cue. As Mason (1972, p. 75) has commented, senate agendas "tend to be exceedingly crowded, . . . [and] even if a senator has succeeded in placing a policy-question in the agenda 'it will not be reached until the meeting has gone on so long that the member's one overwhelming desire is to go home' " (Duff and Berdahl, 1966). As a result, not every item that is proposed for the senate agenda actually gets on it, and not every item that gets on it is attended to. The presence of a specific item on an agenda that becomes the subject of extended discussion and possible action therefore signifies that it is of unusual importance and worth an investment of administrative time. By the same token, a matter proposed to the senate but not considered by it can be used as a justification for administrative indifference. The senate thus operates in the university in a manner similar to that of a public agency before a budget subcommittee. When there are no more than the usual level of complaints, no action need be taken. But when "an agency shouts more loudly than usual, . . . subcommittee members have a pretty good idea that something is wrong" (Wildavsky, 1974, p. 154).

Because most items that someone wants discussed by the senate are never acted on, the use of the senate as an attention cue is an efficient way of allocating attention. It relieves the administration of responsibility for dealing with every problem, establishes a rationale for a system of priorities, provides a justification for inattention to some items, and maintains the symbolic relationship of administration responsiveness to faculty concerns.

The Senate as a Personnel Screening Device. Universities constantly have to fill administrative positions, and it is often less disruptive institutionally as well as more desirable financially to do so with faculty members. However, not every faculty member is acceptable, and at least two characteristics not often found in combination are desirable: A person should have the confidence of faculty colleagues and should also be sympathetic to the administrative point of view. The senate provides a forum in which such persons can be more easily identified and evaluated.

Election to the senate itself provides strong (although not absolutely reliable) evidence of acceptability to faculty colleagues, and working with administrators in preparing reports or other committee assignments allows senators to demonstrate through the equivalent of on-the-job participation their commitment to administrative values.

Anecdotal evidence indicates that administrators are often selected from among faculty "committeemen" (Ladd and Lipset, 1973, p. 83), and case study material (Deegan and Mortimer, 1970; McConnell, 1971) has shown how the intimate involvement of faculty committee members with administrative officers in policy formulation has meant that "many senate committee members have moved easily and naturally into regular administrative positions" (McConnell, 1971, p. 103). Of course, persons selected for administrative positions because they perform well in ideological and noninstrumental debates of the senate may turn out not to be the most effective institutional leaders (Cohen and March, 1974).

The Senate as Organizational Conservator. More attention has traditionally been given to the presumed negative consequences of the university's acknowledged resistance to change than to the potentially positive aspects of maintaining the ongoing system. From a functional perspective, ongoing organizational processes and structures exist in an equilibrium that is a response to and a resultant of forces operating on and within the institution. As with any open system, the university is homeostatic in nature and tends to react to the instability caused by change by responding in a manner that returns it to its former state. The senate, by inhibiting the propensity to change that increasingly characterizes the administration, serves as a major element in this homeostatic process of organizational conservation.

Administrators in general, and presidents in particular, usually do not wish to change the university in dramatic ways, and in fact, the processes through which they are selected and socialized tend to make their roles conservative (Cohen and March, 1974). Yet they occupy boundary positions in the organization and find themselves exposed, as faculty members are not, to the demands of the external environment as well as those of the organization. In that external environment, there are a number of factors that implicitly or explicitly pressure university administrators to become more intrusive in organizational life (see, for example, Keller, 1983). Administrators may attempt to introduce new institutional policies in response to regulations enacted or proposed by state agencies, calls for accountability by external study groups, or potential fiscal emergencies based on worst-case scenarios. These policies almost always seek to increase administrative authority. Faculty are less likely to be directly influenced by such pressures and therefore less likely to be persuaded that dramatic action is required. By opposing such initiatives, senates not only act as "an effective mechanism for restricting centralized control over academic programs" (Blau, 1973, p. 164) but also serve as a constraint on an ambitious administration (Dykes, 1968).

In addition to external pressures, there are powerful, if less obvious, reasons for increased administrative activism, and these reasons are related to the increased availability of institutional information. The movement toward the "management" of higher education has, among other things, led to complex systems for the administration's collection and analysis of previously inaccessible institutional data. These data illuminate anomalies, inequities, and nonstandard practices that must then be justified or abolished and therefore provoke administrative intervention. But as Trow (1975) has pointed out, it is precisely the obscurity caused by bad data collection that may permit the diversity and innovation on which institutional quality is based. The senate's ability to resist administrative initiatives can therefore be seen, at least in some cases, as protecting the institution from making changes based on measurable but ultimately unimportant factors and thus preserving those enduring organizational and institutional qualities that are beyond routine measurement.

In addition to the increased quantity of data, there are also changes in the processes through which data reach administrators in executive positions, as well as in the speed with which they move through the organization. In the past, data might eventually have come to administrative attention after having first been passed through and manipulated by a series of committees and long after corrective administrative measures could be applied. Today these same data may be transmitted directly to the president from a state coordinating board, often with a time lag measured in weeks rather than years. The effect on a university can be similar to that in other social systems characterized by "symptoms of communication failures based on a superabundance of information, inadequately assimilated, rather than its scarcity" (Douglas Cater, cited in Magarrell, 1980, p. 1). Today's administrators may face an endless and often real-time stream of data calling for corrective action before there is time to plan, consult, or fully consider.

The existence of a senate reduces administrative aspirations for change and increases the caution with which the administration acts. This not only protects much of value within the organization but also prevents the unwitting disruption of ongoing but latent systems through which the university keeps the behavior of organizational participants within acceptable bounds. The senate thus is the structure through which, in Clark Kerr's (1963, p. 100) terms, the faculty serve as the institution's balance wheel, "resisting some things that should be resisted, insisting on more thorough discussion of some things that should be more thoroughly discussed, delaying some developments where delay gives time to adjust more gracefully to the inevitable. All this yields a greater sense of order and stability."

The Senate as Ritual and as Pastime. Senates usually meet on a regular schedule, follow a standard agenda format, involve the same core of participants, and engage in their activities under stipulated rules of order. In an organization typified by ambiguity, it is often comforting to engage in scheduled and structured activities in which the behaviors of others can be generally predicted. The senate thus serves as a ritual, a "formality of procedure or action that either is not directed towards a pragmatic end, or if so directed, will fail to achieve the intended aim" (Burnett, 1969, p. 3). The identification of the senate as "theatrical and debate-oriented" (Keller, 1983, p. 127) underscores its ritualistic qualities.

The rituals of senates serve a number of important organizational functions. Among other things, rituals help stabilize and order the organization, provide assurances that mutually expected interactions will occur, and reduce anxiety (Masland, 1983). Senates also provide organizational participants with opportunities for engaging in acceptable behavior when faced with ambiguous or uncertain stimuli. When one doesn't know what else to do, participating in senate debate can appear to be a contribution toward solutions and can enable faculty members to "pretend that they are doing something significant" (Baldridge, Curtis, Ecker, and Riley, 1978, p. 80).

Ritual provides participants with a sense of membership and integration into an organization and into a profession. For others, however, the senate may be enjoyed purely as a pastime. It is a place where one can meet friends, engage in political intrigues, gossip about the administration, and complain about parking—all common forms of faculty recreation. It is also a place where speeches can be made, power can be displayed, nits can be picked, and the intricacies of Robert's Rules of Order can be explored at infinite depth. Those faculty who do enjoy such things have a vested interest in perpetuating the senate, for without it a forum for their involvement would be lost.

The Senate as Scapegoat. The best laid plans of institutions often go awry. To some extent, this may be caused by cognitive limits that suggest that only a small proportion of potentially important variables may be attended to at any given time. Equally important may be the organizational characteristics of colleges and universities as decentralized and loosely coupled systems (Weick, 1976). In such systems, it is often difficult to predict events, and intentions, actions, and outcomes may be only modestly related. Even the power of the president, usually considered the single most influential person in the institution, is severely circumscribed.

When plans are not enacted or goals not achieved, organizational constituents search for reasons. To meet psychological needs, these reasons must of course blame others and not oneself; and to meet political needs, these reasons must be specific rather than conceptual. A president is unlikely to blame an institutional failure on weak presidential performance, and a board of trustees is not likely to accept a president's argument that a certain task cannot be performed because it is beyond the capabilities of a loosely coupled system. On the other hand, boards can understand a president's assertion that a specific act was made difficult or impossible because of opposition by the senate and may even entertain a claim that it would be impossible to implement a program because of the likelihood of future senate opposition. In the same way, faculty members at the department or school level can argue against considering a new policy on the grounds that the senate would not approve it and can blame the senate when a program supported by the senate breaks down when implemented at lower organizational levels.

Cause-and-effect relationships are extremely difficult to assess in the equivocal environment of the college or university. The actions (or lack thereof) of a structure such as the senate, which has high visibility and an ambiguous charge, can plausibly be blamed for deficiencies of all kinds in institutional operations. An academic department can use the senate as a scapegoat for its own unwillingness to make the difficult choices necessary to strengthen its departmental curriculum, and a politically incompetent president can accuse it of scuttling a major policy initiative. In these and similar cases, the senate helps the participants "make sense" of an exceptionally complex system while at the same time preserving their self-images of acumen and professional competence.

Academic Senates in Symbolic Organizational Systems

This chapter began by discussing the perceived shortcomings of senates when traditional organizational models of the bureaucracy, collegium, and political system are used to assess their effectiveness. It then suggested a number of important latent functions that senates may play. Let us now consider these latent functions in the context of newer models that view organizations as symbolic or cultural systems.

Our world is too complex, equivocal, and confusing to be understood completely, and people must find ways of simplifying and interpreting it if they are to function effectively. There are many ways in which the world can be interpreted, and organizations can be seen as groups of people who interact regularly in an attempt to construct and understand reality, to make sense of ambiguous events, and to share meanings in distinctive ways. Through their regular interactions, they develop a culture, which may be defined as "the values or social ideals and the beliefs that organizational members come to share. These values or beliefs are manifested by symbolic devices such as myths, rituals, stories, legends, and specialized language" (Smircich, 1983, p. 344).

Within the context of these cultural inventions, people decide what is important, take indeterminate relationships and develop them into coherent beliefs about cause and effect, and retrospectively make sense of events that were too equivocal to be understood as they occurred. A major organizational model built on these ideas is that of the "organized anarchy," an institution characterized by problematic goals, unclear technology, and fluid participation. "The American college or university is a prototypical organized anarchy. It does not know what it is doing. Its goals are either vague or in dispute. Its technology is familiar but not understood. Its major participants wander in and out of the organization. These factors do not make the university a bad organization, or a disorganized one; but they do make it a problem to describe, understand, and lead" (Cohen and March, 1974, p. 3).

An organized anarchy is a loosely coupled system in which individuals and subunits within the organization make essentially autonomous decisions. Institutional outcomes are a result of these only modestly interdependent activities and are often neither planned nor predictable. It is difficult in such an environment to make inferences about cause and effect, to determine how successful one is, or even to be certain in advance whether certain environmental changes or evolving issues will turn out to be important or trivial. In this situation of great ambiguity, people spend more time in sense making than in decision making (Weick, 1979) and in engaging in activities that verify their status. The decoupling of choices and outcomes makes symbolic behavior particularly important, and particular choices, problems, solutions, and participants often become associated with one another because of their temporal, rather than their logical, relationships.

Organized anarchies need structures and processes that symbolically reinforce their espoused values, that provide opportunities for individuals to assert and confirm their status, and that allow people to understand to which of many competing claims on their attention they should respond. They require a means through which irrelevant problems and participants can be encouraged to seek alternative ways of expressing themselves so that decision makers can do their jobs. They should also be able to "keep people busy, occasionally entertain them, give them a variety of experiences, keep them off the streets, provide pretexts for storytelling, and allow socializing" (Weick, 1979, p. 264).

Given these requirements, the issue of the "success" of the academic senate can be seen from a completely different perspective. Questions concerning its rationality, efficiency, ability to resolve important issues, representativeness, and community-building effectiveness, which may be important under other models, are of less consequence here. If one uses notions of symbolic or cultural systems to consider a college or university as an organized anarchy, academic senates may be effective indeed. This may be the reason they have survived and prospered even though they have not fulfilled the manifest purposes that their charters claim. If senates did not exist, we would have to invent them.

It is time to say something nice about senates. The concept of organized anarchy appears to capture a significant aspect of the role of the senate on many campuses but certainly not of all senates on all campuses at all times. There are many examples of senates that have taken responsibility for resolving a specific problem and have done so in a timely and efficient manner. There are senates in which important institutional policy has been determined and through whose processes of interaction faculty have developed shared values and increased feelings of community. Given the comments of observers of the senate, however, these appear to be exceptional, rather than common, occurrences.

Those who observe the workings of senates and find them deficient should be particularly careful in making recommendations for change, because these changes might affect not only performance of manifest functions but their important latent functions as well. This is particularly true when making recommendations based on normative and ultimately moral concepts such as shared authority or representativeness. Merton (1957, p. 71) warned that "since moral evaluations in a society tend to be largely in terms of the manifest consequences of a practice or code, we should be prepared to find that analysis in terms of latent functions at times runs counter to prevailing moral evaluations. For it does not follow that the latent functions will operate in the same fashion as the manifest consequences which are ordinarily the basis of these judgments."

Anyone who recommends that senates change or be eliminated in favor of some other organizational structure should carefully consider their latent functions. As a general principle, "any attempt to eliminate an existing social structure without providing adequate alternative structures for fulfilling the functions previously fulfilled by the abolished organization is doomed to failure [and] is to indulge in social ritual rather than social engineering" (Merton, 1957, 81). Functional analysis also enables us to evaluate more clearly those warnings about senates, such as that senates are "ineffective because faculty [are] not active participants. If faculty do not become involved in . . . senate . . . affairs, the ominous predictions about the demise of faculty governance may come true" (Baldridge and Kemerer, 1976, p. 410). To the extent that the organized anarchy model is an appropriate one, the future of the senate in governance is unlikely to be related to increased faculty involvement.

References

American Association for Higher Education. *Faculty Participation in Academic Governance.* Washington, D.C.: American Association for Higher Education, 1967.

Baldridge, J. V. "Shared Governance: A Fable About the Lost Magic Kingdom." *Academe,* 1982, *68,* 12–15.

Baldridge, J. V., and Kemerer, F. R. "Academic Senates and Faculty Collective Bargaining." *Journal of Higher Education,* 1976, *47,* 391–411.

Baldridge, J. V., Kemerer, F. R., and Associates. *Assessing the Impact of Faculty Collective Bargaining.* AAHE-ERIC Higher Education Research Report No. 8. Washington, D.C.: American Association for Higher Education, 1981.

Baldridge, J. V., Curtis, D. V., Ecker, G., and Riley, G. L. *Policy Making and Effective Leadership: A National Study of Academic Management.* San Francisco: Jossey-Bass, 1978.

Begin, J. P. "Faculty Collective Bargaining and Faculty Reward Systems." In L. Becker (ed.), *Academic Rewards in Higher Education.* Cambridge, Mass.: Ballinger, 1979.

Ben-David, J. *American Higher Education: Directions Old and New.* New York: McGraw-Hill, 1972.

Blau, P. M. *The Organization of Academic Work.* New York: Wiley, 1973.

Burnett, J. H. "Ceremony, Rites, and Economy in the Student System of an American High School." *Human Organization,* 1969, *28,* 1–10.

Carnegie Commission on Higher Education. *Governance of Higher Education: Six Priority Problems.* New York: McGraw-Hill, 1973.

Carnegie Foundation for the Advancement of Teaching. "A Governance Framework for Higher Education." *Educational Record,* 1983, *64,* 12–18.

Cohen, M. D., and March, J. G. *Leadership and Ambiguity: The American College President.* New York: McGraw-Hill, 1974.

Cohen, M. D., and March, J. G. "Decisions, Presidents, and Status." In J. G. March and J. P. Olsen (eds.), *Ambiguity and Choice in Organizations.* (2nd ed.) Bergen, Norway: Universitetsforlaget, 1979.

Cohen, M. D., March, J. G., and Olsen, J. P. "A Garbage Can Model of Organizational Choice." *Administrative Science Quarterly,* 1972, *17,* 1–25.

Corson, J. J. *Governance of Colleges and Universities.* New York: McGraw-Hill, 1960.

Deegan, W. L., and Mortimer, K. P. *Faculty in Governance at the University of Minnesota.* Berkeley: Center for Research and Development in Higher Education, University of California, 1970.

Deutsch, M. *The Resolution of Conflict: Constructive and Destructive Forces.* New Haven, Conn.: Yale University Press, 1973.

Duff, J., and Berdahl, R. *University Government in Canada.* Toronto, Canada: University of Toronto Press, 1966.

Dykes, A. R. *Faculty Participation in Academic Decision Making.* Washington, D.C.: American Council on Education, 1968.

Etzioni, A. *Modern Organizations.* Englewood Cliffs, N.J.: Prentice-Hall, 1964.

Feldman, M. S., and March, J. G. "Information in Organizations as Signal and Symbol." *Administrative Science Quarterly,* 1981, *26,* 171–186.

Floyd, C. E. *Faculty Participation in Decision Making: Necessity or Luxury?* ASHE-ERIC Higher Education Report No. 8. Washington, D.C.: Association for the Study of Higher Education, 1985.

Hobbs, W. C. "Organizational Roles of University Committees." *Research in Higher Education,* 1975, *3,* 233–242.

Hodgkinson, H. L. *The Campus Senate: Experiment in Democracy.* Berkeley, Calif.: Center for Research and Development in Higher Education, 1974.

Keller, G. *Academic Strategy: The Management Revolution in American Higher Education.* Baltimore, Md.: Johns Hopkins University Press, 1983.

Kemerer, F. R., and Baldridge, J. V. *Unions on Campus: A National Study of the Consequences of Faculty Bargaining.* San Francisco: Jossey-Bass, 1975.

Kerr, C. *The Uses of the University.* Cambridge, Mass.: Harvard University Press, 1963.

Ladd, E. C., Jr., and Lipset, S. M. *Professors, Unions, and American Higher Education.* Washington, D.C.: American Enterprise Institute for Public Policy Research, 1973.

Lieberman, M. "Representational Systems in Higher Education." In S. Elam and M. H. Moskow (eds.), *Employment Relations in Higher Education.* Washington, D.C.: Phi Delta Kappa, 1969.

McConnell, T. R. "Faculty Government." In H. L. Hodgkinson and L. R. Meeth (eds.), *Power and Authority: Transformation of Campus Governance.* San Francisco: Jossey-Bass, 1971.

McConnell, T. R., and Mortimer, K. P. *The Faculty in University Governance.* Berkeley: Center for Research and Development in Higher Education, University of California, 1971.

Magarrell, J. "The Social Repercussions of an 'Information Society'." *Chronicle of Higher Education,* 1980, *20,* 1, 10.

Masland, A. T. "Simulators, Myth, and Ritual in Higher Education." *Research in Higher Education,* 1983, *18,* 161–177.

Mason, H. L. *College and University Government: A Handbook of Principle and Practice.* New Orleans, La.: Tulane University, 1972.

Merton, R. K. *Social Theory and Social Structure.* (Rev. ed.) New York: Free Press, 1957.

Millett, J. D. *The Academic Community.* New York: McGraw-Hill, 1962.

Millett, J. D. *New Structures of Campus Power: Successes and Failures of Emerging Forms of Institutional Governance.* San Francisco: Jossey-Bass, 1978.

Mortimer, K. P., and McConnell, T. R. *Sharing Authority Effectively: Participation, Interaction, and Discretion.* San Francisco: Jossey-Bass, 1978.

Smircich, L. "Concepts of Cultural and Organizational Analysis." *Administrative Science Quarterly,* 1983, *28,* 339–358.

Stone, J. N., Jr. "Achieving Broad-Based Leadership." In R. W. Heyns (ed.), *Leadership for Higher Education.* Washington, D.C.: American Council on Education, 1977.

Tierney, W. G. "Governance by Conversation: An Essay on the Structure, Function, and Communicative Codes of a Faculty Senate." *Human Organization,* 1983, *42,* 172–177.

Trow, M. "The Public and Private Lives of Higher Education." *Daedalus,* 1975, *104,* 113–127.

Veblen, T. *The Higher Learning in America.* New York: Sagamore Press, 1957. (Originally published 1918.)

Weick, K. E. "Educational Organizations as Loosely Coupled Systems." *Administrative Science Quarterly,* 1976, *21,* 1–19.

Weick, K. E. *The Social Psychology of Organizing.* (2nd ed.) Reading, Mass.: Addison-Wesley, 1979.

Wildavsky, A. *The Politics of the Budgetary Process.* (2nd ed.) Boston: Little, Brown, 1974.

Robert Birnbaum is professor of higher education at the University of Maryland, College Park.

Data from a national survey indicate that 91 percent of colleges and universities have a participative governance body that includes faculty and that both faculty and administrative leaders find these bodies effective and useful.

Participative Governance Bodies in Higher Education: Report of a National Study

Joseph E. Gilmour, Jr.

The last two years have seen a resurgence of interest in participative governance bodies in higher education. (Participative governance bodies are defined here as campus governance units with a faculty majority. They include academic senates, academic councils, faculty bodies of the whole, and more broadly representative organizations that have administrator, student, and/or nonacademic staff members.) The American Association for Higher Education (AAHE) held sessions on faculty governance at recent annual meetings, including national symposia in 1989 and 1990, and plans additional programs in the future. In his keynote address to the 1989 symposium, Stanley O. Ikenberry, president of the University of Illinois, stated: "Faculty participation in the governance of universities is important. . . . It grows out of an acknowledgment of the special character of the academic enterprise. . . . Shared governance . . . works imperfectly and needs to be strengthened . . . [and it] can grow stronger if we make a commitment . . . to make it happen." Discussions at these AAHE sessions and a review of the literature show clearly that there is a lack of current information on participative governance body structure, operations, and effectiveness. Almost all of the available research—McConnell and Mortimer (1971); Dill (1971); Millett (1978); the Stanford Project on Academic Governance (Kemerer and Baldridge, 1975; Baldridge and others, 1978; Baldridge, Kemerer, and Associates, 1981; Kemerer and Baldridge, 1981); the American

The author wishes to thank the Lilly Endowment for its support of this project.

Association of University Professors Committee T (1971); Adler (1977); and Berdahl and Edelstein (1983)—was completed over a decade ago.

This chapter reports on a national study of participative governance body organization and operations designed to fill this void. The study addressed several questions: (1) How are participative governance bodies organized, how do they operate, and what support do they receive? (2) What is the relation of these governance bodies to the collective bargaining unit at their institution? (3) How are these bodies perceived by their chairs and institution presidents? (4) What important issues have these bodies addressed in the past three years, and what issues do they plan to undertake over the next three? (5) How could these bodies be strengthened? The study was designed primarily to assist faculty and institutional leaders in the design and review of participative governance structures at their institutions.

Methodology and Data Sources

The study utilized a questionnaire survey constructed for presidents and governance body chairs. The chair's form was substantially longer because most of the information about senate organization and operations was sought from this group. The president's form contained fewer items that focused on this group's perceptions of their governance bodies. These items, however, were virtually the same as those contained in the chair's form.

Both surveys were mailed to the president's office with a request that the chair's form be directed to the appropriate person and that the president or the institutional officer with principal liaison responsibilities with the governance body fill out the president's form. After four weeks, one-third of the institutions that had not responded were called to ascertain why. No problems with the procedure were found. At the fifth week, a second set of surveys was mailed with a follow-up letter.

Survey forms were mailed to a stratified sample of 800 institutions, and the 402 responses yielded a 50.2 percent response rate. Institutions from nine Carnegie categories were represented. All research I and II and doctorate-granting I and II institutions were included in the sample. Random samples were drawn from comprehensive I and II (35 percent sampled), liberal arts I (54 percent sampled) and II (34 percent sampled), and two-year colleges (15 percent sampled). The overall response rate was respectable for survey research using mail questionnaires and is comparable to response rates for similar types of surveys (for example, Baldridge, Kemerer, and Associates, 1981). Response rates in the individual Carnegie categories ranged from 77 percent for research II institutions to 30 percent for the two-year colleges. The data concerning the two-year colleges must be interpreted cautiously because of the low response rate for that category.

Summary statistics were computed for all items on both the president's and chair's questionnaires. Chi square analyses were completed to test for differences in item responses based on Carnegie classification, collective bargaining, institutional control, and institutional size. Two-tailed t tests for differences in percentages between overall mean scores and group subscores were computed from groupings in which the chi square statistic was significant at the .05 level or less. No significant differences were found between institutions that bargained collectively and those that did not, or between independent and public colleges and universities. For this reason, this chapter does not focus on these groupings.

Results

Governance Body Organization, Operations, and Support. Ninety-one percent of the 402 institutions responding to the survey had a participative governance body. Two-year colleges were significantly less likely to have one; only 73 percent reported having such a body. Eighty-four percent of these governance bodies were representative structures. The presence of such structures was related to institutional size. Ninety-eight percent of the institutions with more than 10,000 students had such organizational arrangements, while only 64 percent of colleges with less than 2,000 students had them.

Participative governance bodies at the institutions surveyed averaged 58 seats and had a median of 44 seats. There was a curvilinear relationship between the number of seats and institutional size: The mean for colleges with less than 2,000 students was 55 members; for 2,000 to 10,000 students, 43 members; for 10,000 to 20,000 students, 48 members; and for greater than 20,000 students, 106 members. As Table 1 shows, the bodies were faculty dominated. All counted full-time faculty in their membership. Fifty-nine percent had administrators, and approximately one-quarter included part-time faculty, professional staff, and undergraduate students. Fewer contained graduate students or classified staff. Liberal arts I and II college

Table 1. Composition of Governance Body Membership

Membership Category	Percent Governance Bodies Including	Mean Number of Seats	Median Number of Seats
Full-time faculty	100	45	38
Part-time faculty	23	*	*
Administrators	59	11	6
Professional staff	25	9	4
Classified staff	7	4	2
Graduate students	12	6	2
Undergraduate students	28	8	3
Overall		58	44

*Data reported too inconsistently to compute.

governance bodies were significantly more likely than average to have part-time faculty members, with 41 and 56 percent, respectively. Research I and II institutions were significantly more likely to have undergraduate and graduate student members; in both cases, approximately 45 percent had them. Nonfaculty groups were enfranchised at 79 percent of the institutions.

Fifty-two percent of the governance bodies surveyed had the word *senate* in their name, 18 percent were referred to as the *faculty*, 17 percent as *council*, and 13 percent by some other name. Sixty-eight percent met monthly, and 15 percent convened biweekly. The remaining 17 percent gathered semiannually, quarterly, or weekly. Forty-one percent had an annual budget with an average size of $36,900 and a median level of $5,000. The presence of a budget was related to institutional size; 74 percent of the institutions with enrollments greater than 10,000 had a budget.

Most governance bodies kept records of their proceedings. Ninety-eight percent kept summary minutes; 61 percent, tape recordings; 42 percent, verbatim minutes; and 52 percent distributed newsletters on their activities. With regard to meeting agendas, 97 percent of the survey respondents indicated that faculty contributed agenda items "much" or "some" of the time, as compared to 85 percent for administrators, 27 percent for students, and 21 percent for institutional board members.

Executive Committee Organization and Operation. Seventy-three percent of the participative governance bodies surveyed had an executive committee with an average of eight seats. The presence of such committees was size related: 47 percent of institutions with enrollments under 2,000 students had an executive committee, while 97 percent of institutions with enrollments greater than 20,000 had them. As Table 2 shows, 94 percent had full-time faculty and approximately a quarter had administrators and undergraduate students in their membership. Ten percent or less included part-time faculty, professional and classified staff, and graduate students on the committee. Research I institutions (39 percent) were significantly more

Table 2. Composition of Executive Committee Membership

Membership Category	Percent Committees Including	Mean Number of Seats	Median Number of Seats
Full-time faculty	94	8	7
Part-time faculty	10	7	6
Administrators	29	2	2
Professional staff	8	2	1
Classified staff	4	5	7
Graduate students	9	3	2
Undergraduate students	20	2	1
Overall		8	7

likely to have graduate students on their executive committees. With the exception of administrators, who held their seats by virtue of their position, executive committee members were elected most frequently by the governance body (46 percent of the time) or by the faculty at large (28 percent).

The principal roles played by executive committees were to prepare an agenda for the governance body (84 percent) and to meet with the president or academic vice-president (76 percent). In approximately 60 percent of the cases, the executive committee also decided on legislation, functioned for the governance body when the institution was not in session, established committees and defined their charges, and appointed committee members. Of considerably less importance as roles for these committees were dispute mediation and meeting with governing boards.

Standing Committees. Table 3 reveals that the standing and ad hoc committees of the participative governance bodies surveyed focus on the academic and faculty affairs functions traditionally reserved for these bodies. It also shows some movement into management areas such as budgeting and planning, administrator review, and representation on major search committees. Survey respondents were asked to indicate the authority (determinant, formal recommendation, and informal advice) assigned to each of the areas in which their governance body's standing or ad hoc committees operated. In the majority of areas, the committees provided formal recommendations.

Table 3. Areas in Which Governance Body Standing or Ad Hoc Committees Have Responsibility, and the Level of Authority in Those Areas

| | Percent Having Committee | Level of Authority | | |
Governance Area		Determinant	Formal Recommendation	Informal Advice
Academic Affairs				
Curriculum	87	20	75	5
Degree requirements	78	24	71	5
Course approval	71	30	63	7
New education programs	76	18	74	8
Admissions	68	19	47	34
Calendar	65	16	59	26
Research policy	50	18	71	21
Faculty Affairs	86	19	72	11
Student Affairs	66	5	47	48
Management Issues				
Budget and planning	76	–	49	51
Staff affairs	32	1	25	74
Administrator review	42	2	51	46
Search committees	57	4	65	31

Governance Body Chairs. Sixty-seven percent of the faculty governance bodies surveyed were chaired by an elected officer. Another 17 percent were led by the president, and 11 percent were overseen by the academic vice-president. Liberal arts I institutions (46 percent) and research I institutions (33 percent) were significantly more likely to be chaired by the president. Where the chair was elected, the governance body voted in 56 percent of the cases and the faculty as a whole selected the chair 36 percent of the time. The chair served for one year in 84 percent of the bodies that elect and for two years in the remaining 16 percent. A few institutions noted that they had established a three-year rotation in which the chair started as chair-elect in the first year, assumed the chair in the second, and finished the final year as immediate past chair.

Table 4 shows the type of institutional support available to governance body chairs and committee chairs. As might be expected, the level of support available to governance body chairs was greater than that for committee heads. Phone service, secretarial support, and staff assistance from campus administrative offices were available to a sizable majority of governance body chairs. Over 40 percent received travel, release time, and office space. Less than 20 percent had an executive secretary or a stipend. Committee chairs were provided phone service, secretarial support, and staff assistance from the institution administration 40 percent or more of the time. There was a relationship between size and the support available: 71 percent of the chairs at institutions with enrollments greater than 10,000 were provided release time; 75 percent at institutions with greater than 20,000 received space; 42 percent with enrollments greater than 20,000 had an executive secretary; and 92 percent at these same large universities had secretarial assistance.

Relationship with Collective Bargaining Unit. Twenty-one percent of the institutions surveyed had a collective bargaining unit. The presence of such units was significantly more prevalent at institutions of between

Table 4. Types of Support and Percentage of Institutions Providing Such Support to Governance Body Chairs and Committee Chairs

Items	Governance Body Chair	Committee Chair
Phone service	73	49
Travel	44	15
Stipend	11	3
Release time	44	11
Office space	43	13
Secretarial support	72	46
Executive secretary	19	7
Staff support from administrative offices	63	40

10,000 and 20,000 students, where 35 percent had such organizations. Collective bargaining was also more likely at research II, comprehensive I, and two-year institutions and less likely at research I, doctorate-granting I, and liberal arts I institutions. In 60 percent of the cases, where there was collective bargaining, the governance body was recognized in the contract. Seventy-eight percent of the time, the relationship between the collective bargaining unit and the governance body was complementary or actively supportive. In 14 percent of the cases, it was separate or uninvolved; in another 4 percent, it was adversarial; and in the remaining 4 percent, it was "other."

Perceptions of the Participative Governance Body. Respondents were asked to agree or disagree with a number of statements about their participative governance bodies using a four-point Likert scale. Table 5 shows the percentage of agreement and strong agreement with these statements by governance body chairs and presidents. The level of agreement between the two groups was striking; in only four variables was the difference greater than 10 percent. These differences were in the expected directions: The presidents agreed more with positive statements about areas

Table 5. Perceptions of Participative Governance Bodies

	Percent Agreeing with Statement[a]	
Governance Statements	Chairs	Presidents
Administrative Support		
1. Represented in policy bodies	78	86
2. Members rewarded for service	37	57
3. Operating budget adequate	61	73
4. Involved in important decisions	83	89
5. Management information available	90	95
Communication		
6. Communicate well with administration	92	91
7. Communicate well with board	70	75
8. Meet regularly with administration	88	94
9. Meet regularly with board	50	39
10. Agree on governance body role	65	67
Performance		
11. Represents faculty point of view	93	85
12. Operates efficiently	78	69
13. Attracts capable people	69	57
14. Has sufficient information	84	83
15. Practices adhere to constitution	100	95
16. Attracts good committee members	63	65
17. Obtains quorum easily	83	77
18. Leaders are well prepared	83	75
19. Considers important issues	92	93
20. Governance body runs satisfactorily	76	78
Performance Composite	82	78

[a] Percent agreement and strong agreement have been combined.

for which they had responsibility—rewards to members for service, providing an adequate operating budget—and disagreed more with statements about the regularity of governance body meetings with the institution board and the capacity of their bodies to attract capable people. The chairs' perceptions were the reverse.

There were lower levels of agreement (below 70 percent from either chairs and/or presidents) with positive statements about the presence of capable people on the governance body and its committees, the sufficiency of rewards for service, the extent to which administration and faculty leaders share role expectations for the governance body, the efficiency of body operations, and the adequacy of operating budgets. The governance body Composite Performance Index (the means of items 11 to 20 in Table 5) was 79 percent (weighted) for chairs and presidents combined.

There were some patterns of differences in the perceptions of senate chairs based on institutional types. The responses of senate chairs in five Carnegie classifications (research I and II, doctorate-granting I, comprehensive I, and liberal arts II) to most of the seventeen items in Table 5 were close to the percentages shown. However, there were four Carnegie types (doctorate-granting II, comprehensive II, two-year, and liberal arts I) at which the chair's response on five or more of the twenty items differed from the average by at least 10 percentage points. The deviations from the average ratings for chairs in these four institutional categories are shown in Table 6. Doctorate-granting II, comprehensive II, and two-year institutions had consistently lower scores across the full spectrum of variables. Liberal arts I colleges, on the other hand, provided more positive than average ratings across the spectrum. If there was a pattern, it was that support and communication variables correlated with performance levels.

Most Important Issues. Study respondents were asked to list the five most important issues their governance body had addressed in the past three years and five most important to be addressed in the next three. Table 7 shows the ten top-ranked issues identified by the respondents in both time frames. Management issues were an important part of the agenda for the governance bodies surveyed for both the past and the next three years. Overall, the rankings of the chairs and the presidents were closely related; for issues addressed in the last three years, the two groups selected the same issues for their top four and ranked them identically and also had eight of the same issues in the top ten. For issues to be addressed in the next three years, parallel rankings were provided for the top three issues, and again, eight of the top ten issues overlapped. The issues of minority issues and assessment, which did not appear in the "Addressed" column, were in the "To Be Addressed" column. Other than these, however, the issues addressed for the last and next three years coincided to some degree; four issues overlapped for the presidents and seven for the chairs.

Table 6. Differences of More than Ten Percentage Points in Perceptions of Chairs in Four Institution Types

Governance Statements	Type of Institution[a]				
	All Types	Doc II	Comp II	2-Yr	LA I
Administrative Support					
1. Represented in policy bodies	78	–	–28	–17	+15
2. Members rewarded for service	37	–17	–	–	+23
3. Operating budget adequate	61	–	–36	–14	+16
4. Involved in important decisions	83	–	–19	–12	+13
5. Management information available	90	–23	–	–	–
Communication					
6. Communicate well with administration	92	–12	–12	–11	–
7. Meet regularly with administration	89	–	–15	–	–
8. Agree on governance body role	65	–35	–32	–	+24
Performance					
9. Represents faculty point of view	93	–	–	–13	–
10. Attracts capable people	69	–	–15	–	+25
11. Has sufficient information	83	–	–	–	+13
12. Practices adhere to constitution	100	–10	–	–	–
13. Attracts good committee members	63	–	–	–	+15
14. Obtains quorum easily	83	–	–16	–	–
15. Leaders well prepared	83	–23	–	–15	–
16. Considers important issues	92	–	–	–10	–
17. Governance body runs satisfactorily	76	–26	–19	–	–

Note: Percent agreement and strong agreement have been combined.

[a] Doc II = doctorate-granting II institutions, Comp II = comprehensive II colleges, 2-Yr = two-year colleges, and LA I = liberal arts I colleges.

Table 7. Top Issues of Presidents and Governance Chairs

Rank	Presidents	Rank	Chairs
	Addressed in the Past Three Years		
1	Planning, budget, mission		Planning, budget, mission
2	Benefits, personnel policies		Benefits, personnel policies
3	Faculty issues		Faculty issues
4	Curriculum		Curriculum
5	Salaries, compensation		New programs
6	General education core		Salaries, compensation
7	New programs		Institutional governance
8	Institutional governance		General education core
9	Academic standards		Governance body organization
10	Calendar		Student affairs/athletics
	To Be Addressed in the Next Three Years		
1	Planning, budget, mission		Planning, budget, mission
2	Faculty issues		Faculty issues
3	Curriculum		Curriculum
4	Assessment		Governance body organization
5.5	General education core	5	Minority issues
5.5	Other	6	General education core
7.5	Governance body organization	7	Salaries, compensation
7.5	Minority issues	8	Assessment
9	Program termination		Other
10	Admissions, enrollment		New programs

Table 8. Ways in Which
Participative Governance Body Could Be Strengthened

Rank	Presidents	Rank	Chairs
1	Strengthen governance body organization and operations		Strengthen governance body organization and operations
2	Greater participation by members		Greater financial and secretarial support
3	Greater focus on major issues		Greater participation by members
4	Attract more capable members		Better collaboration
5	Better collaboration		Increase governance body powers
6	Improve communication		Greater participation incentives
7	Involve more faculty		Attract more capable members
8.5	Greater accountability	8	Greater focus on major issues
8.5	Greater participation incentives	9	Improve communication
11.5	Members better prepared	10	Involve more faculty
11.5	Greater financial and secretarial support		
11.5	More positive relations with collective bargaining unit		

Ways to Strengthen Participative Governance Bodies. Table 8 lists areas in which chairs and institution presidents believed governance body performance could be improved. Although there were different rankings, there was considerable overlap in areas identified by the two groups. However, they had a tendency to rank issues pertaining to the other's performance as needing greater improvement than their own. For example, presidents ranked "greater focus on major issues" by the governance body number 3, while the chairs ranked it 8. Conversely, chairs ranked "greater financial and secretarial support" number 2, while the presidents ranked it 11.5.

Conclusion

A high proportion (91 percent) of the institutions surveyed had a participative governance body. Only the two-year colleges differed significantly from this norm, with 73 percent reporting the presence of such a body on their campuses. Overall perceptions of governance bodies held by presidents and chairs were good; 79 percent agreed or strongly agreed with positive performance statements about their body, suggesting that they believed that it played an important governance role with relative effectiveness. This result needs to be interpreted cautiously, however, since both groups had a vested interest in their participative governance body. Nevertheless, it suggests a more optimistic view than that reported by the Stanford Project on Academic Governance and by Birnbaum (this volume) who contended that academic senates did not work well as participative governance bodies, but did serve useful latent organizational functions. One institution type, liberal arts I, outshone all others on administrative support, communication, and performance variables. The study did not clearly point to a reason for this, but the traditions of excellence and strong faculty governance at these institutions may account for this result.

On the negative side, respondents indicated that members were not sufficiently rewarded for service to the governance body, that operating budgets were inadequate, that the most able faculty were not attracted as members or for committee service, and that their body did not operate efficiently. These perceptions were echoed in respondent comments on how governance bodies could be strengthened. Respondents ranked three needs highest: enhancement of governance body organization and operations, greater member participation, and increased financial and secretarial support. These negative perceptions were particularly pronounced at doctorate-granting II, comprehensive II, and two-year institutions, where inadequate support from the administration and poor communications apparently led to lower levels of performance.

Size and Structure. Study results revealed that a key variable differentiating participative governance body structure was institutional size. A curvilinear relationship was found between enrollments and the size of the governing body. This was because at many institutions with less than 2,000 students, the governance body was the entire faculty, while at institutions with more than 2,000 students, representative bodies generally ran from relatively small committees to progressively larger ones in relation to enrollments. Colleges with enrollments of less than 2,000 students were also less likely to have an executive committee or an operating budget for their governance body. For institutions enrolling more than 20,000 students, the executive committee of the governance body was likely to have a larger and more powerful role, and the chair was likely to be better supported by the institution.

Additional Conclusions Relating to the Literature. It appears that the trend toward multiconstituency bodies in which students and staff were added in the early 1970s to bring college communities closer together has waned. The Stanford Project on Academic Governance reported in its 1971 and 1974 surveys (Baldridge, Curtis, Ecker, and Riley, 1978) that 50 percent of the institutions included had students on their governance body and almost one-third had staff. This study found that students were members in 28 percent of the cases and staff in 25 percent.

The study results also revealed that the level of faculty participation in policy-making has increased somewhat and the issue areas in which governance bodies are operating has expanded. From a level of "consultation" reported by the American Association of University Professors Committee T (1971) and Adler (1977), the governance bodies have increased their influence to "formal recommendation" for most issues. In addition, the issues on which the governance bodies have been working have expanded to include economic and management issues not traditionally in their province.

Collective bargaining did not appear to be the threat perceived by McConnell and Mortimer (1971) and instead was in keeping with Adler's (1977) and the Stanford Governance Project's (Baldridge, Kemerer, and Associates, 1981) conclusion that governance bodies and collective bargaining units can coexist. It is, however, more likely to occur at institutions with 10,000 to 20,000 students and at research II, comprehensive I, and two-year institutions and less likely to be present at research I, doctorate-granting I, and liberal arts I universities and colleges.

Need for Further Research. There are many issues that this study did not address because of its descriptive design. For example, how do successful senates position themselves to play a significant role in institutional policy-making? How do supportive administrations help their senates to be effective? How do successful senates organize themselves to do their work, what kinds of support staff are required, and how do they maintain continuity in their operations over the years? These issues can best be addressed in a series of in-depth case studies of successful participative governance bodies drawn from each of the Carnegie institutional types.

Higher education governance researchers should undertake to study these questions in a concerted way in the not-too-distant future.

References

Adler, D. L. *Governance and Collective Bargaining in Four-Year Institutions 1970–1977.* Academic Collective Bargaining Information Service Monograph No. 3. Washington, D.C.: Academic Collective Bargaining Information Service, 1977.

American Association of University Professors Committee T. "Report of the Survey Subcommittee of Committee T." *AAUP Bulletin,* Spring 1971, pp. 68–124.

Baldridge, J. V., Curtis, D. V., Ecker, D., and Riley, G. L. *Policy Making and Effective Leadership.* San Francisco: Jossey-Bass, 1978.

Baldridge, J. V., Kemerer, F. R., and Associates. *Assessing the Impact of Faculty Collective Bargaining.* AAHE-ERIC/Higher Education Research Report No. 8. Washington, D.C.: American Association of Higher Education, 1981.

Berdahl, R. O., and Edelstein, S. "Perceptions and Practice: A Maryland Survey on Governance." In E. Sumler (ed.), *The Faculty Role in Governance: Proceedings of a Statewide Conference in Maryland.* Annapolis, Md.: Institute for Research in Higher and Adult Education, University of Maryland and the Maryland State Board of Higher Education, 1983.

Dill, D. D. *Case Studies in University Governance.* Washington, D.C.: National Association of State Universities and Land Grant Colleges, 1971.

Kemerer, F. R., and Baldridge, J. V. *Unions on Campus.* San Francisco: Jossey-Bass, 1975.

Kemerer, F. R., and Baldridge, J. V. "Senates and Unions: Unexpected Peaceful Coexistence." *Journal of Higher Education,* 1981, 52 (3), 256–264.

McConnell, T. R., and Mortimer, K. P. *The Faculty in University Governance.* Berkeley: Center for Research and Development in Higher Education, University of California, 1971.

Millett, J. D. *New Structures of Campus Power: Successes and Failures of Emerging Forms of Institutional Governance.* San Francisco: Jossey-Bass, 1978.

Joseph E. (Tim) Gilmour, Jr., is executive assistant to the president and vice-president for strategic planning at the Georgia Institute of Technology.

Case studies of the dynamics of campus governance indicate that the effectiveness of academic senates depends on structure, culture, and administrative posture toward faculty involvement in institutional decision making.

Campus Leaders and Campus Senates

Barbara A. Lee

Surveys of faculty attitudes toward campus governance conducted over the past three decades have revealed a consistent theme: Faculty are dissatisfied with the quality, quantity, and outcome of their involvement beyond the department level in academic governance (American Association for Higher Education, 1967; Ladd and Lipset, 1975; Mortimer, Gunne, and Leslie, 1976; Carnegie Foundation for the Advancement of Teaching, 1982). Although little systematic information is available about the attitudes of academic administrators toward governance, it is safe to say that they, too, are unhappy with campus governance, although often for different reasons. Despite variations in the issues facing higher education over the years—from increases to declines in enrollment, from student activism to apathy, from glutted faculty job markets to faculty shortages—governance problems have been seemingly impervious to resolution.

The interplay between leadership and governance is of special importance at times when institutions are under stress, whether they are facing financial difficulty, the need to adapt to a changing student population, or pressure to perform more efficiently or effectively. A governance system on a campus is usually in place when a leader (president, provost, or dean) arrives, and the leader must decide whether to work within the existing governance system (both formal and informal), attempt to modify it, or completely restructure it. Irrespective of the alternative selected, the gover-

This study was prepared pursuant to a grant from the Office of Educational Research and Improvement/Department of Education (OERI/ED). However, the opinions expressed herein do not necessarily reflect the position or policy of the OERI/ED, and no official endorsement by the OERI/ED should be inferred.

41

nance system may pose a formidable constraint on the leader's ability to effect change.

The research discussed in this chapter reports the results of visits to eight institutions of higher education where data were collected on the interplay between leadership and governance and, more specifically, on how leadership both affected governance and was affected by it. The eight institutions were a subset of a larger sample of thirty-two institutions participating in the Institutional Leadership Project, a five-year longitudinal study sponsored by the National Center for Postsecondary Governance and Finance. The eight institutions included two universities (one public, one private), two state colleges recently renamed "university," two private comprehensive colleges, and two public community colleges. Respondents included presidents, provosts, other vice-presidents, deans, department chairs, faculty senate leaders, union leaders, and faculty not formally involved in the senate. Because the focus was campus-level governance and, more particularly, the interaction between faculty and administration through the operation of the governance system, the term *leadership* was broadly defined. It included both academic administrators (the president and the provost or similar position) and faculty governance representatives.

What Is Governance?

For purposes of this study, governance was defined as the way that issues affecting the entire institution, or one or more components thereof, are decided. It included the structure, both formal and informal, of decision-making groups and the relationships between and among those groups and individuals. It included the process used to reach decisions and the outcome of recommendations from governance groups to higher-level individuals or groups. The governance "system" (and, more particularly, the institution's senate) and how it affected and was affected by leadership was the focus of attention.

The number, role, and interaction of governance groups vary by institution or campus, but most governance systems have a campuswide body such as a senate or faculty council. It is this group and its relationship with academic administrators and other significant faculty organizations (such as a faculty union) that this chapter examines. Although senates have a number of roles and purposes, this chapter does not attempt to evaluate whether the senate's role was appropriate or whether it was fulfilling that role (Millett, 1978). The senate's role and function on each campus were taken as a given; this research assessed the characteristics of senates and the apparent effects of those characteristics on each senate's perceived effectiveness, as well as the reciprocal relationship between senates and leaders.

Both faculty and administrators value senates, although for different reasons (Birnbaum, this volume). While some argue that the value of a senate is primarily symbolic (Millett, 1978; Birnbaum, this volume), others assert that a senate can play a significant role in managing a college or university (American Association for Higher Education, 1967). Yet others commend a faculty role in governance so that administrators will have "someone with whom to share the blame for mistakes" (Keller, 1983, p. 61). Given the substantial amount of time, energy, attention, and nurturing that is needed to create and maintain an academic governance system, senates are obviously perceived either as useful or as a necessary evil. Because senates are unlikely to "go away" (Birnbaum, this volume), assessing the characteristics of useful senates as well as senates that are necessary evils should enhance our understanding of how senates and academic leaders function within a governance system.

Characteristics of Senates

Senates on the eight campuses differed in their perceived effectiveness and credibility with faculty and administrators. There is much literature on organizational effectiveness (for example, Cameron, 1978); it is beyond the scope of this chapter to define effective governance or to attempt to explain why faculty and administrators believe that a certain governance system is effective or ineffective. In this chapter, perceived effectiveness is an expression of a positive view of the governance system by both faculty and administrators and a belief that little or no change in the system is needed. Analysis of both the functional and dysfunctional governance systems revealed three dimensions that appeared to contribute to a system's perceived effectiveness. These are the system's broadly defined structure, the cultural context in which the system operated, and the interaction between the faculty governance structure and the administration. Each of these contributed to the system's perceived effectiveness. Several of the elements emerging from the eight campus visits were also included in a national study of faculty governance systems (Gilmour, this volume). Although the survey data were not available until the research described in this chapter was completed, the Gilmour data confirm or supplement several findings of the field research.

Structural Issues. The single most important structural issue in the governance system's perceived effectiveness was its composition, including the identity of its chair. Senates that included large numbers of nonfaculty (this category includes academic administrators) were viewed by both faculty and administrators as less effective than faculty-dominated or all-faculty bodies. Gilmour (this volume) found that nearly two-thirds (59 percent) of all senates included administrators as members and that students and professional staff were members of approximately one-fourth of the senates. In the present study, one institution was attempting to add nonfaculty professionals to the senate, and the faculty were furious at the usurpation of their primacy in the senate. At another institution in this study, the senate was chaired by the president, while the senates of five institutions were chaired by faculty. At the institution where the president chaired the senate, the faculty did not believe that the senate represented their views or was a legitimate faculty governance vehicle.

Another important issue encompassed the size and complexity of the senate. At one institution, the senate had thirty-one committees, leading to numerous disagreements about which committee should deal with certain issues, while at another institution where governance was perceived to be effective, there were only three standing senate committees. Respondents reported that it was difficult to staff a large number of committees with faculty who would devote the necessary time and attention to committee work. It seemed that greater senate size and complexity resulted in the perception of inefficiency, leading in turn to a perception of the senate's ineffectiveness.

A third structural element that affected a senate's perceived effectiveness was the composition and role of its executive committee. Because of the size of most senates, the executive committee did the most important work of the senate—setting the agenda, often determining committee assignments (both members and issues), framing issues for presentation to the body, and cutting deals with the administration. Gilmour's (this volume) study found that 73 percent of the senates had an executive committee, and of these, 84 percent set the senate agenda, 76 percent met with the president or provost, and 60 percent established and appointed committee members. At the institution where the president chaired the senate, there was no executive committee and thus no ability for faculty and administrative leaders to discuss important issues informally or shape issues collaboratively. The senate was viewed as illegitimate by faculty on that campus. How the executive committee saw its role and how it was perceived by the senate itself clearly contributed to the senate's perceived effectiveness.

Closely related to the composition of the executive committee was the agenda-setting process. As noted previously, at institutions where a president or provost set the agenda nearly unilaterally, the faculty viewed the senate as illegitimate. On the other hand, if the faculty controlled the agenda completely, the probability was high that issues important to the administration would either not be addressed or would be deferred indefinitely.

The way that issues were framed for the senate, and by whom, was also important, particularly at institutions preparing for substantial change in mission, size, or quality standards. Unilateral framing of issues, either by administrators or faculty, was often counterproductive; interaction between the two groups, either through the executive committee or a more informal mechanism, was perceived to produce better-quality decisions with less lengthy deliberation.

The boundaries of the senate role, particularly on campuses where faculty were unionized, were less important than expected. Although early writing about faculty bargaining predicted that unions would either destroy senates or usurp their functions, research on dual-track governance has found, instead, that unions play a protective role vis-à-vis the senate, often because the leadership overlaps (Baldridge and Kemerer, 1976; Lee, 1979). Gilmour's study (this volume) found no difference, in either the presence of a senate or its characteristics, between unionized and nonunionized campuses. In the research conducted for this study, little evidence of role conflict with the union was found, although occasionally, administrators and senates disagreed on the proper boundaries for the senate (and it was not necessarily the faculty seeking to expand the senate's role).

In sum, structural elements were important primarily because they influenced the way that the senate functioned and its ability to deal with complex issues. While poorly functioning senates were not solely a result of structural problems, it would be difficult for a senate to function well if the structure militated against it.

Cultural Issues. The impact of an institution's culture on its values, structure, and priorities has been well documented (Masland, 1985; Chaffee and Tierney, 1988). For senates, as well, the cultural context in which they operated had important effects on their functioning. One of the most dramatic and obvious cultural elements was the governance history of the institution. On several campuses, old disputes between long-gone provosts or presidents and the faculty had shaped the governance system in ways that even two or more decades could not change. At one campus, widespread faculty distrust of an unpopular president focused the faculty on the process, almost to the exclusion of the outcome, of any governance issue. The cultural context shaped the posture of the senate leadership; on that campus it was guardian of the process and the status quo, while on others it was a positive agent for change.

Another contextual factor that influences governance is the faculty's attitude toward the senate. A senate viewed as illegitimate, for structural or other reasons, is not viewed as an attractive leadership opportunity for faculty. Often the faculty's attitude toward the senate is shaped not by the characteristics of its leaders but by the way the administration responds to it.

A third cultural element that is viewed as critical to governance effectiveness is the quality of faculty who choose to participate. Although administrators on some campuses complained that only faculty with axes to grind or who were poor researchers or teachers participated in governance, this was not true across the eight institutions. Some respondents noted that the quality of senate leadership varied with the intensity of faculty emotions about certain issues in certain years, with the better leaders being energized by anger over an issue. Birnbaum (this volume) has noted that views of administrators toward the senate are often influenced by their attitudes toward its leaders. In Gilmour's data (this volume), administrators were less likely than the senate chairs to believe that the senate's leaders were "capable people," although only 69 percent of the chairs believed that the senate attracted capable people. It is difficult to separate this element from the others in this section and even more difficult to trace cause-and-effect relationships between the quality of faculty leadership and the way that faculty leaders are treated by academic administrators.

A critical factor to a governance system's success, and one that was not addressed satisfactorily on any of the eight campuses, was the development of leadership continuity. At best, a president-elect served for a year as the president's assistant. At worst, offices turned over annually with little communication between new and old officers, no attempts by leaders (either faculty or administrative) to help new officers learn their roles, and inadequate exploitation of the knowledge of former officers. At institutions where the senate was perceived to be functioning appropriately, more attention was given to continuity, but surprisingly, only minimal efforts were made to provide information, training, or advice to prospective or new officers, even on the good governance campuses.

Administrative Posture. The third dimension of governance systems found to be critical to perceived effectiveness was the posture of the president and/or provost toward the system. The degree to which the administration permitted the system to operate, the amount of interaction between faculty governance leaders and top administrators, and the responsiveness of top administration to recommendations from the governance group shaped faculty and administrative attitudes toward the legitimacy and effectiveness of the system.

Although it might be expected that an important component of an effective senate would be the commitment of institutional resources to senate use, the data did not support this conjecture. Gilmour (this volume) found that 44 percent of senate chairs received release time, 72 percent of senates were given secretarial support and telephone service, and 43 percent were given office space. In Lee's study, all but one institution gave the senate an office, at least a part-time secretary, a telephone, and release time for its officers, but there were substantial differences in perceived effectiveness of senates among these institutions. It may be that senates need institutional resources in order to function at a minimal level of effectiveness but that such resources do not predict that a senate will be perceived as effective.

On campuses where governance was viewed as relatively effective, there was a routinized formal relationship between faculty governance leaders and the administration. On several campuses, this involved inviting the senate chair (and on one campus, the chair-elect also) to all presidential cabinet meetings. Depending on the campus, the senate chair gained access to confidential and often sensitive information and provided a faculty voice at the cabinet level. Inclusion of the senate chair, on occasion and depending on the chair, was also used as a co-optation device. On one campus, it became the custom for senate officers to sit with an administrative committee that advised the provost on promotion and tenure recommendations. The faculty were not permitted to participate in the discussion or to vote, but their presence at these meetings increased the faculty's confidence in the fairness of personnel decisions and promoted trust between the governance leaders and top administrators.

An important supplement to the formal relationship was an informal relationship between the senate chair and either the president or the provost. If the president had a limited internal role in governance, then the senate chair's relationship with the provost was the important element. Regular interaction appeared to result in greater trust and more inclination on the part of both sides to resolve problems informally.

Most important in this dimension was top administration's deference to the governance system for most issues that affected the academic core of the institution or the faculty's welfare. This does not mean that the administration always accepted faculty recommendations, but that it allowed the senate to deal with any issue within the senate's purview, whether it was a matter of institutional survival or a trivial matter. Although several presidents reserved to themselves and their administrative team the responsibility for long-range planning, on those campuses where governance was perceived to be effective, administrators shared the outline of plans with governance leaders, and the implementation of the plans was delegated to the faculty governance structure.

Another important feature of governance relationships perceived to be effective was the administration's accountability to the senate. The "batting average" for faculty recommendations was less important here than the administration's practice of explaining why, on occasion, it could not accept the senate's recommendation, or why it felt that some modification was necessary. On some campuses, the administration worked with the senate to achieve the modifications the administration believed necessary. On those campuses where senate leaders were included in the administrative cabinet, the need to reject or modify senate recommendations was infrequent.

The administration's deference to the governance system and inclusion of its leaders in institutional management was either facilitated or constrained by the other two dimensions: the governance structure and the institutional governance culture. Administrative attempts to defer to the governance system were hampered by negative cultures or overly complex structures, and of course, negative cultures were created in the first place by faculty perceptions that administrators were unwilling to defer to the governance structure. This intertwining of the three dimensions made it difficult for either faculty leaders or administrators to improve governance relationships that had been historically poor, but on those campuses where all three dimensions were favorable, it resulted in a governance system that was viewed as relatively effective (to the degree that any such system can be so viewed).

An Assessment of Three Senates

Of the eight institutions visited, two institutions had no campuswide governance system, which caused serious communication problems among academic units. Another had a governance structure so atypical that its analysis would not be useful to other institutions. A fourth had a governance structure created completely by collective bargaining agreement, a structure that addressed only curricular matters and left all other governance issues to the union contract. A fifth was in the process of changing its structure to reduce the number of committees and to add nonfaculty representatives.

Of the remaining three institutions, one had a governance system that both faculty and administrators viewed as reasonably effective. The governance system of the second could be safely characterized as paralyzed. A third had a governance system that could be characterized as "troubled" because its cultural context was the stumbling block. We will now describe the senates on these three campuses using the framework developed in the previous section.

Respecting the System

Structure. Urban College (UC) is a large, comprehensive public institution with a wide range of programs. The basic governance structure is the faculty senate, which is the executive body of the faculty assembly (all full-time faculty) and consists of four officers and twelve additional senators elected from the academic divisions. No administrators serve on the senate or meet with it regularly. One counselor attends meetings but may not vote. The senate has three committees: one for personnel decisions, one for minor resource allocation decisions, and a third for academic matters (including curriculum issues).

There are other bodies with responsibilities that overlap some of the senate's: for example, an instructional council (which includes senators, deans, and chairs) that handles curriculum matters and an academic council that deals with instructional concerns and consists of a large number of administrators and chairs. The provost meets with the senate executive committee regularly to set the agenda and help shape the issues to be addressed. There is no faculty union; in fact, it was clear that the president's decision to defer all academic and faculty status matters to the senate was a union-avoidance technique. No instances of administrative failure to respect the senate's purview were reported.

Culture. UC, although founded over a century ago, was fortunate from a governance standpoint that it attained its present size and complexity, as well as most of its faculty, within the past decade. The current president arrived at that time and created the governance system; he has supported and encouraged the faculty's governance role ever since.

Although the faculty supported the senate and viewed it as legitimate, many believed that the administration did not pay enough attention to faculty views. There was no dispute, however, over the credibility of the senate.

With regard to the quality of faculty leaders, one senior administrator believed that faculty complacency with the governance system resulted in the selection of mediocre leaders. According to this administrator, "The weakest thing [about governance at UC] is that faculty put a low priority on the senate and governance, and they are willing to elect less than the best faculty for leadership roles. This makes working with the senate more difficult for the administration. The faculty feel that they're treated fairly already, so it doesn't matter who the senate president is." No system was in place for the continuity of senate leadership. The senate chair met regularly with the provost and somewhat less regularly with the president, and despite the fact that the chair-elect was designated a year in advance, only the current chair dealt with top administrators. This lack of attention to leadership continuity may have contributed to the perceived poor quality of senate leadership.

Administrative Posture. Although administrative support for the faculty governance system at UC was strong and consistent, it was motivated by pragmatism rather than ideals. A senior administrator disparaged faculty governance, saying, "With the rapid change facing higher education today, I have some real doubts about the ability of academic governance to succeed. Governance focuses on keeping the status quo." But this distaste for faculty governance was exceeded by a distaste for faculty unions, and the administrator viewed deference to faculty governance as a quid pro quo for union avoidance.

Although another senior administrator's support for governance was consistent with institutional policy, the expressed attitude was completely different: "The ability to effect change is difficult in a mature organization with very powerful faculty. It takes patience if you want the faculty to come along with you. I would rather take longer and have the faculty on board than push something through." The senate chair is a member of the president's cabinet (a forty-member body that includes various administrators, support staff, and students). The chair does not meet with the president's council (the vice-presidents and the president). The cabinet is an information-sharing group; the senate chair had asked to attend president's council meetings but had been rebuffed.

Informal meetings between the senate chair and top administrators are frequent; the chair meets weekly with the provost and at least monthly with the president. The chair reported that both administrators were always available and that the president encouraged even more frequent meetings.

The administration's commitment to the senate is evident in its allocation of resources for senate use. The chair receives a 40 percent teaching reduction, the chair-elect receives approximately a 15 percent reduction, and the senate secretary receives approximately a 6 percent reduction. The senate has a budget, an office, a telephone, and the unlimited use of the provost's clerical staff. Although assigning the provost's secretary to the senate appears to be a conflict of interest, the provost stated that the secretary maintained the confidentiality of senate material.

Administrative deference to the senate's role was reported to be high and consistent. A faculty leader asserted that neither the president nor the provost would permit "end runs" but would insist that the matter be taken up by the senate. Although the faculty leader remarked that "the administration does look at the senate as a necessary entity that needs to be" and viewed its motives as political rather than normative, both sides reported that the system worked well.

The studied deference of administrators to the governance system was reflected in their accountability to the system. Only one faculty recommendation—on salary levels—had been rejected by the administration in recent years. The low level of conflict between the senate and the administration appeared to be a result of the substantial informal interaction between the senate chair and other senate leaders and top administrators. A senior administrator remarked, "It's important that they [the senate] be perceived as legitimate and effective," and the administration's policy was calculated to that end.

Although perceived as reasonably effective, respondents at UC were not without criticism of the governance system. Some faculty criticized the structure as too complex and lengthy (a curriculum matter, for example, would be addressed by five layers of groups or individuals). Senior administrators criticized its slowness, and one viewed his role as "developing a sense of urgency for issues" because the system took so long to resolve a problem. Nevertheless, top administrators viewed their acceptance of and deference to the senate as critical to responding to their constituency, improving quality, and avoiding a faculty union.

A System Paralyzed

Structure. System College (SC) is part of a major state university system with a systemwide governance code. The code requires that the senate include only faculty and that it develop recommendations on matters of academic concern and faculty welfare.

SC's president is an ex officio member of the senate and attends meetings and makes reports but does not chair the meetings (as the former president did). Although the code gives the president the power to appoint all committee members, he has delegated that power to the executive committee. Twenty-nine standing committees (at a college employing 500 faculty) report to five councils that report to the senate. There are also numerous ad hoc committees. Both faculty and administrators were critical of the senate's structure as overly bureaucratic—a system that "gets in the way of communication."

The president meets regularly with the senate executive committee to set the senate agenda, to shape issues for senate action, and to encourage the officers to take a stronger leadership role. There is no faculty union (although one may be developing), so the senate's purview is broad.

Culture. SC's culture is the governance albatross. Former presidents ran the college as a patriarchy, and the faculty, until now, has been given no real governance role. The senate under previous presidents was the president's captive—chaired by the president and dominated by administrators. Faculty are now expected to participate fully in institutional governance; however, they say they do not know how. Senior administrators are impatient with the faculty's know-nothing attitude and criticize the senate and its leadership for being ineffective.

The faculty's attitude toward the senate is equally critical. A long-time faculty member remarked:

> My largest criticism of the faculty senate is that it continues to operate under [the prior] constraints even though there has been an open invitation from the president to take part in the governance of the institution. It may be the goldfish bowl syndrome—when goldfish who have spent their lives in a goldfish bowl are put in a stream, they still swim in a circle. Mostly senate committee members do what they're supposed to do, but others don't get around to it with the alacrity that they should. Another problem with the faculty senate is that too many people are elected who aren't wholly committed to the work of the senate and the institution—who will be present and prompt. Sometimes there is no quorum, so the senate cannot do its work.

Another faculty member criticized the senate for not communicating with the faculty. He said, "The faculty senate here works better than it used to, but there is little communication between the senate and the faculty. At my former institution, the senate minutes were typed and distributed to all faculty. I said in a faculty meeting that we should get a report from senators, but it is not yet being done." This faculty member put the blame squarely on the senate. He believed that the faculty finally had an opportunity to participate in governance but were squandering it.

The criticism of the senate extends to its leadership as well, although the criticism is less severe. Respondents seemed to recognize that the leaders were fighting a difficult and unsuccessful battle to stir the demoralized senators into effective action. An administrator said, "I have more faith in the faculty governance system than those inside it do. The senate leaders really need help." A senate leader admitted that personal efforts had not been successful: "Senate committees won't study these problems. I can't seem to generate the kind of movement that the senate needs. Committee chairs need to be more active. For example, take the faculty evaluation form [that is used to determine pay increases]. The faculty have been dissatisfied with it for five years, and the senate still hasn't revised it. At a time when change has to occur quickly, resistance slows it down."

There is little attention to leadership continuity at SC. Although the senate chair is involved in many committees (discussed in the next section), the chair-elect is not. In fact, the chair-elect is selected in April and takes office in May, so there is no time for sensitizing or training the chair-elect.

The faculty's inexperience in governance and the former patriarchal culture of the institution were cited by every respondent as the reason for the system's paralysis. Although everyone agreed on the reason for the dysfunction, no one suggested interventions, such as training, retreats, or other mechanisms to boost faculty expertise and confidence in their governance role. Everyone blamed people who were gone (former presidents) and bemoaned the result, while failing to move ahead with the critical matter of building a system that could work.

Administrative Posture. A senior administrator simultaneously expressed hope and frustration with the governance system. In an effort to avoid dominating the senate, the administration has insisted that the senate solve its own problems, revise its own structure, and begin addressing important issues in a timely way. The situation is especially grave because SC is under considerable external pressure to raise its admission standards, improve its curriculum, and enhance the performance of its students. This external pressure exacerbates the senate's paralysis because many faculty are resisting these changes.

The president has established several formal settings for interaction with the senate chair. The chair is invited to the president's meetings with the vice-presidents, and the college's planning committee includes the senate chair. Furthermore, the president meets regularly with the senate chair and the executive committee.

Informal meetings are also frequent and usually initiated by the administration. One administrator said, "My relationship with the senate is probably more trusting than they may be comfortable with. I have regular heart-to-heart talks with the senate chair." The chair confirmed that administrators were always available and were very supportive.

The administration has provided resources for the senate—an office, a telephone, a part-time secretary, and three hours of release time, a 25 percent reduction. No release time is provided for the chair-elect, since that person is only in that role for one month.

The administration has made it clear that it expects the senate to perform its role and has refused to make the faculty's decisions for them. But simultaneously, the administration is pressured to make major changes in the curriculum, student quality, and student outcomes to comply with state requirements. This pressure has led administrators, frustrated with the senate's paralysis, to create other governance structures to deal with some issues or to make the decisions without the senate. This behavior, of course, reinforces the paralysis of the senate and permits the doubting faculty to point fingers at autocratic administrators. A faculty leader concluded that the college needs "marriage counseling" to help all groups deal with conflict and resolve it. This leader said, "We need more tolerance by both administrators and faculty. They [administration] have to realize that [change] is not going to happen overnight. There is so much impatience and frustration. Some decisions are painful. The faculty are turned off by being told that they are the problem. The administration is in too much of a hurry." A relatively new administrator agreed with this assessment, replying, "There are several faculty who have their Mary Kay or real estate businesses and spend minimal time on campus. But there are others, especially a group of older faculty, who really want to try, but they don't understand that the rules have changed. There are some new faculty who are pretty good or very good, but they're reacting badly to the president's strategies because his management tactics are aimed at the lowest group of faculty. The good faculty are insulted, and they'll either retreat into their shells or will leave if they get a better offer."

At SC, all three dimensions of the governance system contribute to its paralysis. Its structure is overly complex and bureaucratic, its culture is not conducive to faculty confidence in the governance system, and the administration, while evidencing considerable support for the system, has undermined it through its impatience with the system's paralysis. All parties are so busy pointing fingers at each other that little constructive progress is being made to resolve the situation. Particularly when the system is stressed by external pressures for change, the energy devoted to blaming drains the institution's ability to focus on how that change will occur.

A Fixation on Process

Structure. The senate at Rural College (RC) is dominated by faculty, but it also includes all deans, the president and provost, the library director, other nonfaculty members, and six students. Membership totals 62 (the college employs 500 faculty). The senate chair, in recent years always a faculty member, is elected by the senate. The senate addresses all academic matters and has the final say on curriculum matters.

The president attends all senate meetings and makes some initial remarks, but then does not participate in senate discussion. The senate executive committee includes the president, provost, senate officers, and two at-large members. The executive committee sets the agenda, screening issues to determine whether to take them to the senate or drop them. It appoints members to standing committees and creates ad hoc committees as well. It also develops resolutions for senate consideration.

RC faculty have been unionized for two decades, and the boundaries between senate and union turf appear well established. The same people held senate and union office, although usually not concurrently. Although the senate works closely with the president and provost, the union has no relationship with either leader. The union president deals with a member of the business vice-president's staff and has no communication, either formal or informal, with academic administrators. Both union leaders and academic administrators are satisfied with this arrangement.

Culture. The culture of this institution had an important effect on governance. A senior administrator explained, "We recruited a bright, young faculty fifteen years ago, and they got caught in the academic crunch [the stagnant job market]. They had not planned to stay, but they are still here. . . . There is an activist core, made up of faculty from the arts and sciences. They want the college to be different than it is . . . more graduate education and more research and all the trappings that go with research." The college's history was troubled by a series of presidents that the arts and sciences faculty believed to be autocratic. The union was formed in response to faculty dissatisfaction with a president. A faculty leader said, "Atrocity precedes a union. There was an autocratic president who denied raises to people he disliked. The AAUP [American Association of University Professors] censured [the college]. Faculty were fired. The academic senate was reorganized." The senate was reorganized following the censure to remove all administrators except the deans, provost, and president. Although the union has survived one decertification attempt, the union leadership acknowledged that it would not call a strike, because the faculty would not support it.

Subsequent presidents were also reported to be insufficiently deferential to faculty concerns or recommendations (one administrator described former presidents as "strong-arm, benevolent dictators"). In recent years, the board of trustees' rejection of a faculty search committee recommendation for a new president outraged faculty and nearly destroyed the governance system. The college's history of troubled governance has resulted in a faculty that is focused on guarding the governance process, while substantive issues are of secondary importance. An administrator described the governance culture as one of intense faculty interest in the minutiae of decision making. For example, he said, "Faculty spend hours allocating peanuts [small amounts of dollars] for faculty travel."

The faculty view the senate as critical to maintaining a strong voice in institutional matters. Faculty support for the senate is so strong that administrators know better than to attempt to circumvent it. One said, "The faculty is *very* interested in governance. The academic senate is very important. I wouldn't dream of doing anything about curriculum—that's their territory." Conversations with both faculty and administrators suggested that it was the system the faculty valued, not the outcomes or the way the system dealt with issues.

Because the system was the faculty's focus, there was less pressure on faculty leaders to be effective. An administrator criticized senate leaders, saying, "The faculty leadership that emerges, I have found, is not the best and the brightest of the faculty. It is made up of those who love the intrigue of faculty governance, who are politically active. The faculty abdicated the senate leadership to a small arts and sciences group a long time ago. They [faculty] would all have more clout if the others [beyond arts and sciences] were more involved in leadership functions. . . . I don't think the faculty have good leadership." No other respondents mentioned senate leadership.

Leadership continuity in formal terms is restricted to the election of a chair-elect and the inclusion of the immediate past chair on the senate executive committee. Formal attempts to train or sensitize new leaders may be less important at RC because of the small number of faculty who seek leadership roles and their tendency to hold the same office several times.

Administrative Posture. The formal relationship between the president, provost, and senate chair appears to be confined to meetings of the senate executive committee. The senate chair does not attend meetings of the president's administrative team. Informal meetings, however, are frequent, especially between the provost and the senate chair.

RC provides resources for the senate in the form of an office, a budget, and a secretary. The senate chair gets a 50 percent teaching reduction, but the chair-elect gets no release time.

Administrative deference to the governance system has been noted previously. Because of the college's history and the intensity of faculty interest in protecting the governance process, administrators feel constrained to defer to the process on some issues (for example, personnel decisions or major curricular matters) in which some of them would like to have a stronger voice.

Part of the current president's credibility with the faculty is that the president was selected on the advice of a faculty search committee. In reflecting on the faculty's view of the president, a faculty leader said, "I'm not sure the president himself has made the difference [in governance], or just that he was selected using the proper channels—it's the process that the faculty have primarily reacted to. . . . The processes were developed in the mid 1960s under an unpopular president [and the faculty guard them very jealously]." Because the president was new, it was too early to tell whether the president would continue to defer to the governance system and what the reaction would be if he did not. Furthermore, the college was under no real external pressure to make the kinds of changes that SC was facing, so neither the governance system nor the faculty's relationship with the president were stressed.

Impact of Governance on Leadership

At each of the three colleges included in this chapter, the presidents were respected by the faculty and viewed as strong leaders. UC's president was respected both within and outside the college as a strong advocate for the institution, an effective fund raiser (from both private and state sources), and a creative leader. SC's president was respected for administrative experience at other institutions and a strong vision for the college. At RC, the president was very new and the faculty's respect was due primarily to the fact that the president was their candidate for the job.

Despite the evident ability of these leaders and the faculty's generally favorable reaction to them, each was constrained, albeit in very different ways, by the governance system. While one used those constraints to build faculty support for administrative ideas and plans, another' was unable to shock the system into functioning as a partner rather than an impediment. The third was struggling to shift the faculty's concern from guarding the process to dealing with substance.

Although the president at UC lamented the additional time that it took to process issues through the faculty senate, it did not appear that the institution suffered greatly as a result. The college was thriving, had adequate resources, and was viewed as very responsive to community and business needs. While the faculty were not at all fooled by the administration's pragmatic approach to governance, they were supportive of administrative policies and generally viewed the president as an effective leader.

The president at SC was frustrated by the paralysis of the governance system but chose to work around it rather than taking strong measures to heal it. This approach alienated the faculty because of the conflicting messages that the faculty governance system is critical to a high-quality institution but that the low-quality faculty are the reason for the institution's problems. The president did not seem to see that these strategies further weakened the senate. The institution appeared to be on a collision course, and a faculty group had been formed that was discussing unionization, no-confidence votes, and other measures to express the faculty's dismay.

The impact of RC's governance system on its new president was not clear, but it did result in the president's deciding to use the first year at RC as a learning experience rather than attempting to make change right away. The strong faculty concern over process cannot help but slow the pace of change at RC, if, in fact, change occurs at all. Hailing from an institution with a relatively weak faculty role in governance, this president will have to move cautiously, respect the process in all its details, and develop strong informal channels to faculty who are not involved in the formal process if the president expects to effect change.

Impact of Leadership on Senates

This chapter described governance at three colleges, one with a governance system judged by both its members and the researcher to be relatively effective and two with troubled governance systems. To what degree did the president and provost contribute to the relative effectiveness of these governance systems?

Although academic administrators on all three campuses stated their firm commitment to the process, only on one campus did they make good on that commitment. Despite their personal reservations about delegating important college issues to the senate, UC's administrators consistently deferred to the system. They did not create alternatives to the system. They did not openly criticize the system or the effectiveness of its leaders, although they had doubts on both scores. They made it clear that a strong faculty governance system was a sine qua non of a well-managed college.

On the second campus, administrators, while espousing deference to the faculty governance system, took actions that further weakened it and neglected to take steps to strengthen it. Their simultaneous exhortations that the senate assume more responsibility conflicted with the message they were sending that the institution's problems were the faculty's fault. They disparaged the senate members' ability to function without creating ways for them to learn how to function. They created governance mechanisms to deal with matters that the senate had not been able to deal with. While their impatience is understandable in light of the considerable external pressure for institutional change, these administrators' actions simply failed to improve the governance situation and, in fact, added to its problems.

It was really too soon to ascertain what effect the new top administrators at RC would have on the governance system. They were watching and listening, rather than working closely with the system, and faculty leaders were frustrated with administrators' refusal to communicate their plans for the institution. Because of the faculty's emphasis on process, the administrators understood that they first had to win the faculty's trust in their intention to defer to the system before they could try to have an impact on either that system or institutional problems.

How Can Senates Be More Effective?

While a sample of eight institutions is too small to produce valid generalizations about campus governance, observing how these systems operate and the factors that either enhance or impede their work suggest several strategies for campus leaders, both administrative and faculty, to consider. The data also suggest that some factors may be beyond the control of campus leaders and that leaders must find ways to work around these factors if they cannot be changed.

While structure, culture, and administrative posture toward the senate were all found to be important, structure was the least important. Certainly, a senate dominated by administrators, or including a large proportion of nonfaculty, was not supported by faculty, but the mere absence of nonfaculty did not guarantee that a senate would function effectively. A few elements—faculty domination, resources for the senate, and clarity on the boundaries of the senate's role—seemed to play an important role, and their absence could have seriously impeded a senate's work. But much more was needed for a senate to be viewed as reasonably effective by campus actors.

Negative Culture. A negative culture can impede the best-intentioned leaders. On two campuses, well-intentioned leaders were hampered by faculty distrust or fixation on the past. Any attempts to change the system or to pressure the faculty to address serious institutional needs were viewed with suspicion. Faculty at one college simultaneously complained that the administration never listened to them while grousing that they did not know how to participate in governance and the president was pushing them too hard. Faculty at another institution insisted that they participate in all decisions while criticizing the president for not "leading" the institution. Part of the problem at both these institutions may have been an aging faculty made up of locals who had never taught anywhere else. One might speculate that the anticipated increase in faculty retirements (Bowen and Schuster, 1986) and the orientation of younger faculty to research and their disciplines may ease the pressure for substantial faculty involvement. Nevertheless, at many institutions, leaders faced with negative cultures and an aging faculty cadre with little turnover will find it most difficult to build faculty trust and expertise in shared governance.

Respect and Reward Needed. Governance leaders are rarely respected or rewarded. Even on campuses where the system appeared to function reasonably well, both faculty and administrators criticized the quality of faculty governance leaders. They complained that few faculty were active and that the same ones held office almost all of the time. While Birnbaum (this volume) has noted that giving a faculty "troublemaker" a governance role is one way to diffuse some negative energy, some respondents seemed to believe that nearly all governance leaders fit this description. One reason for the difficulty in attracting good governance leaders is that there are few or no rewards for such service. Release time from teaching is very likely inadequate to compensate an individual for the time spent on governance matters. Furthermore, many institutions are shifting their reward systems to emphasize research and publication, and many others have never rewarded service to the institution, through governance or other activities, even to the degree that teaching is rewarded. So there is little incentive for faculty to participate if they are unrewarded and especially if they are criticized for inadequate research because they spent the time on governance instead.

But how can an institution reward governance activity? If the institution's priority is increasing its prestige to external groups by mimicking higher-status research institutions, can it afford to reward faculty whose research productivity is low or nonexistent? And what of those governance leaders who struggle to maintain the status quo, resisting change and stirring up the faculty to protest leaders' efforts to improve quality? Should individuals who work against what the leaders perceive to be the interests of the institution be rewarded for that? And if not, is it politically feasible, or even desirable, for an institution to reward only those leaders who support the administration's efforts?

Tailoring the reward system to encourage higher-quality faculty participation, while superficially appealing, may be more difficult than it sounds. Nevertheless, campus leaders cannot expect to entice productive, respected faculty to assume governance roles if they are either disadvantaged or not rewarded for their participation.

Leadership Development. Governance leaders need training and seasoning. Although the data are not reported here, faculty and administrators were asked to comment on the characteristics of a good faculty leader. Their answers fell into two categories: personal attributes and an understanding of how the system works. If understanding the system is necessary for effective governance participation, how can we expect an individual to chair a senate if that person has not been actively involved in some other leadership role in the senate? While it is likely that many senate chairs had held committee offices or other leadership positions, there was no mechanism on some campuses to sensitize incoming chairs to recent developments, informal agreements, pending concerns, or the dynamics of the chair's relationship with administrative leaders. And because senate leaders generally held office for only one year, the knowledge of the immediate past chair was often tapped only informally and at the initiative of the incoming chair.

While statewide senates or associations of campus senates at the state level helped sensitize leaders to state-level concerns and how they were implemented on other campuses, there appeared to be no formal opportunity to develop future senate leadership. Given the importance to the faculty of their governance role and given administrative recognition of faculty interest in governance, the lack of leadership development is striking.

It would seem that at a minimum, the past senate chair and the incoming chair should work with the current chair for the year that he or she is in office. The past chair can provide important insights to both the current chair and the chair-elect. The chair-elect will have a year of on-the-job training before he or she assumes the chair's position. This system may cost the institution somewhat more in release time, but if the institution's leadership believes that an effective senate is important, it will find the necessary resources.

Consistent Deference. Deference is inconvenient but necessary. Even on the campus where governance appeared relatively effective, administrators bemoaned the need to defer to the faculty governance system. They believed, however, that consistent deference was the key to effective shared governance.

Deference does not mean abdication of the administrative role. On several campuses where the senate made recommendations on all important institutional matters, faculty conceded that the administration had a right to reject faculty recommendations at least occasionally, as long as an explanation was forthcoming. Faculty did not appear to expect the president or provost to agree with them 100 percent of the time; they did expect that their views would be listened to and considered thoughtfully and that administrators would explain their reasons for rejecting a senate recommendation.

Communication for Consensus. Frequent formal and informal communication builds consensus. While simply communicating does not mean that people will agree, the practice of inviting senate chairs to administrative staff meetings and frequent informal meetings seemed to enhance the effectiveness of campus governance. It is likely that these meetings sensitized both parties to each other's concerns and helped shape the way that the senate discussed issues referred by the administration. At UC, the senate chair and provost both noted that they spent many hours discussing issues until both were clear on each other's position, the president's position, and the faculty and administration's view of the college's needs. They believed that a high level of institutional consensus resulted from these discussions.

What Is the Role of Research?

Although several surveys have been conducted on the characteristics of governance structures and the perceptions of senate leaders and administrators on their effectiveness (Kemerer and Baldridge, 1975; Adler, 1977; Gilmour, this volume), it is only through case studies that a researcher can assess the dynamics of the governance system, the factors that enhance or impede its ability to function, and the degree to which faculty and administrators support it. One of the weaknesses of the case-study methodology is its limited generalizability, but case studies of governance are useful because they can identify practices or structures on one campus that may be either adopted or avoided by other institutions with similar cultures, missions, and problems.

Because a campus senate must deal with a multitude of agendas and because of its substantial symbolic role, it may be insufficient to try to study these bodies with tools of rational analysis. Whatever insights are gained from this study of three senates are of limited predictive value, although they may identify weaknesses or good practice that will inform the efforts of other institutions as they struggle to improve shared governance. This is not to say that one should not try to understand academic governance, but that whatever success one has in identifying factors that enhance or impede governance, there is more happening than can be understood or appreciated.

References

Adler, D. L. *Governance and Collective Bargaining in Four-Year Institutions 1970–1977*. Academic Collective Bargaining Information Service Monograph No. 3. Washington, D.C.: Academic Collective Bargaining Information Service, 1977.

American Association for Higher Education. *Faculty Participation in Academic Governance*. Washington, D.C.: American Association for Higher Education, 1967.

Baldridge, J. V., and Kemerer, F. R. "Academic Senates and Faculty Collective Bargaining." *Journal of Higher Education,* 1976, *47,* 391–411.

Bowen, H. R., and Schuster, J. H. *American Professors: A National Resource Imperiled.* New York: Oxford University Press, 1986.

Cameron, K. S. "Measuring Organizational Effectiveness in Institutions of Higher Education." *Administrative Science Quarterly,* 1978, *23,* 604–632.

Carnegie Foundation for the Advancement of Teaching. *The Control of the Campus: A Report on Governance of Higher Education.* Princeton, N.J.: Princeton University Press, 1982.

Chaffee, E. E., and Tierney, W. G. *Collegiate Culture and Leadership Strategies.* New York: American Council on Education/Macmillan, 1988.

Keller, G. *Academic Strategy: The Management Revolution in American Higher Education.* Baltimore, Md.: Johns Hopkins University Press, 1983.

Kemerer, F. R., and Baldridge, J. V. *Unions on Campus.* San Francisco: Jossey-Bass, 1975.

Ladd, E. C., Jr., and Lipset, S. M. *The Divided Academy.* New York: McGraw-Hill, 1975.

Lee, B. A. "Governance at Unionized Four-Year Colleges: Effect on Decision-Making Structure." *Journal of Higher Education,* 1979, *50,* 565–585.

Masland, A. T. "Organizational Culture in the Study of Higher Education." *Review of Higher Education,* 1985, *8,* 157–168.

Millett, J. D. *New Structures of Campus Power: Successes and Failures of Emerging Forms of Institutional Governance.* San Francisco: Jossey-Bass, 1978.

Mortimer, K. P., Gunne, M. G., and Leslie, D. W. "Perceived Legitimacy of Decision Making and Academic Governance Patterns in Higher Education: A Comparative Analysis." *Research in Higher Education,* 1976, *4,* 273–290.

Barbara A. Lee is associate professor of industrial relations and human resources, Rutgers University.

A survey of research universities indicates that faculty do not in general have major roles in resource allocation decisions and suggests the need for reconsidering the concept of "shared authority" to meet the needs of the 1990s.

Faculty Involvement in Institutional Budgeting

John G. Dimond

Faculty participation in the establishment of policies on admission, curriculum, and the hiring, promotion, and evaluation of faculty is widespread in colleges and universities. These areas have long been considered a "primary responsibility" of the faculty (American Association of University Professors . . . , 1984), and the faculty's predominant role in such matters is for the most part unquestioned.

Less frequently noted are recommendations by authoritative groups that the faculty should not be limited to participating in educational decision making but should be included in other critical institutional areas as well, such as budgeting and planning. Such functions are among those assigned to the sphere of "joint effort" in the influential 1966 Statement on Government of Colleges and Universities (American Association of University Professors . . . , 1984). While the concept of "joint effort" was not clearly delineated in that statement, it implied that in the area of planning and budgeting, faculty were expected at least to participate in the exchange of information, to have a voice in determining short- and long-range priorities, and to have access to reports and analyses that could inform their judgment. The importance of faculty participation in resource allocation decisions was made even more explicit by the statement of the American Association of University Professors, Association of Governing Boards, and American Council on Education (1972) on the role of the faculty in budgetary and salary matters. Faculty involvement was justified on the grounds that budgetary decisions ultimately affected academic areas in which the faculty had primary responsibility.

More recently, there have been a number of case studies describing how such faculty participation has been achieved in specific settings (Chan, 1988; Dill and Helm, 1988; Green and Monical, 1985; Lipschutz, 1985; Millett, 1978; Mortimer and McConnell, 1978; Williams, Gore, Broches, and Lostoski, 1987). Many of these studies have noted that the current problems of colleges and universities increasingly call for decisions about institutional direction and for choices among programs and that making such "core" decisions without a high degree of faculty participation may have deleterious effects on institutional morale and on overall effectiveness (Alfred, 1985; Boyer, 1989; Guskin and Bassis, 1985; Hipps, 1982; Mortimer and Caruso, 1984; Pomrenke, 1982; Williams, Gore, Broches, and Lostoski, 1987).

At the same time, some of the case-study reports, as well as other commentators (Plante, 1989), suggest that not much has happened to extend faculty participation in these areas. There are no recent empirical studies that indicate the degree of faculty involvement in institutional resource allocation decisions. This chapter reports on a study of the extent of faculty participation in this area of "joint effort," identifies the mechanisms by which it takes place, and assesses the views of faculty leaders on these modes of participation in public research-based universities. These institutions were selected for the study because they tend to have older and more established faculty governance traditions that are often cited as models for other institutions. If the development of ways to involve faculty in institutional budgeting were to take place relatively smoothly anywhere, it should be within this group of institutions.

Data Sources and Methodology

In 1989, the National Center for Postsecondary Governance and Finance conducted a survey of participative governance bodies (Gilmour, this volume). Data were collected on the structures, powers, and activities of academic senates and on the attitudes of senate leaders and senior administrative officers toward these bodies. Replies were received from 402 institutions, including 65 research universities (Carnegie groups research I and II), of which 52 were public. The public institutions were selected for this study.

Respondents to the Gilmour survey had been asked to indicate whether their academic governance bodies had standing or ad hoc committees in the areas of budgeting and planning and whether they had the power to determine, formally recommend, or informally advise. Of the fifty-two public research institutions, forty-three indicated that they had such committees, twenty-two with "formal recommendation" powers and twenty-one that gave "informal advice." Seven institutions indicated that they had no such committees, and the information available did not allow the remaining two to be classified.

This study determined the extent of actual faculty involvement in institutional budgeting in these institutions through telephone interviews with faculty governance body heads or chairs of faculty budget committees. Initial contact was made at all forty-three institutions identified by Gilmour, and interviews were completed for thirty-nine. Two of these interviews were with senior administrative officers because faculty leaders were unavailable and a president's or provost's office appeared to be taking a relatively strong leadership role in the academic governance body. These thirty-nine institutions constituted the sample for the study.

The interviews were intended to elicit both factual and evaluative information. The following areas were explored:

What were the specific topics of consultation on budget matters over the past few years? For example, did the faculty governance body's agenda include general financial matters, university budget strategy and priorities, university budget allocations, faculty position allocations, or salary practices?

How deeply or extensively were the topics considered?

Was the locus of consultation a senate committee, an administrative committee that included faculty, or a joint consultative body?

What was the frequency of consultation, and was it scheduled or ad hoc?

Was the consultation primarily based on written documents to which reaction was sought, or on oral briefings and general discussion?

What was the outcome of the consultation? Was there a vote or merely a "sense of the meeting"?

Did faculty have adequate notice of topics to be discussed? Was there feedback on the final disposition of the matters under discussion?

In addition to budget matters, did the academic governance system deal with such planning issues as mission statements, university goals, new program priorities, major change or elimination of programs, establishment, major reorganization, or elimination of academic units, capital plans and priorities, or individual building plans?

How satisfied were the faculty with the processes in place?

Were there examples of recent budget matters on which consultation with faculty led to changes?

Would the respondent advocate any particular change in the status quo concerning faculty involvement in institutional budget development?

Results

There were three distinct committee structures through which faculty in the thirty-nine institutions participated in budgeting: committees appointed by the senate or other academic governance body (thirty-five), decision-making committees appointed by administrators (thirteen), and advisory committees appointed by administrators (five). Faculty at twenty-four institutions were represented through membership on one type of committee; faculty at fifteen institutions had membership on two types of committees in various combinations.

In twenty-two institutions (56.4 percent), consultation took place almost exclusively in one or more committees appointed by the senate or other academic governance body. In two institutions (5.1 percent), consultation took place both in a senate-appointed committee and in an administratively appointed advisory committee. In two institutions (5.1 percent), consultation took place solely in administrative advisory committees. In these cases, the senates appointed some of the members of the committee or were consulted by the administration prior to its appointment of members of the committee. Eleven institutions (28.2 percent) had both a senate-appointed budget committee and a faculty presence on the administrative body that made decisions on the overall institutional budget. One institution (2.6 percent) had faculty on an administrative advisory committee plus representation on the administrative decision-making body. One institution (2.6 percent) had no senate or administrative advisory committee, but faculty did have membership on the institutional budget decision-making body.

Extent of Consultation. The roles played in institutional budgeting by the senate and administrative committees with faculty membership varied greatly. The following main categories emerged from the descriptions of the faculty leaders.

Detailed and Comprehensive. The body was consulted regularly and in some detail about the entire institutional budget. Little was off limits, and the body most often saw the final package that the president was recommending to the institution's trustees. Five of the thirty-nine institutions had senate committees that could be described in this way.

Substantial, but Not Comprehensive. The body was consulted extensively and in depth about the budgets of academic divisions, including the library (and in one case about tuition and salary guidelines), but not about the institutional budget as a whole. Two institutions fit this description.

Limited. The body had a specific role with respect to one or more of the following: position allocation, merger or discontinuance of academic programs, cutbacks to be assigned to academic divisions, or additions to academic division budgets for new programs. Faculty committees at the nine institutions that fell into this category appeared not to have a broad involvement in institutional budget matters, but rather were limited to the assigned roles. In some cases, general briefings were given to these bodies on overall budgetary matters, but usually not on any systematic basis.

Salaries Only. The body's main function was to give advice on academic salary policy, salary ranges, division of increases between across the board and merit, and so on. The committees at five institutions fell primarily into this category. While the bodies may have also been briefed from time to time on other budgetary matters, salary issues appeared to be the main focus.

General. The body mainly served as a sounding board for the administration, which conducted briefings on fiscal affairs and from time to time raised matters for discussion. There was little discussion of specific allocations. Seventeen of the thirty-nine institutions fell into this category.

None. The body had no direct role in budget discussion, nor did it appoint faculty to other bodies that did. One institution could be characterized this way, but it had significant faculty presence on the administration's budget committee. In addition, at one of the institutions whose faculty committee concentrated on compensation matters, the senate head perceived this function as so loosely related to budgeting that he felt it was better to say that the senate had no role in the institution's budget making. This institution had a vigorous faculty governance system, which was consulted on such matters as the ranking of new initiatives that were being planned, but not on the ones to which funding should actually be allocated.

Levels of Satisfaction. Those contacted at each institution were asked to indicate their general level of satisfaction with the current arrangements for faculty involvement in institutional budgeting. Replies were grouped into three categories: "highly satisfied," "mixed," and "dissatisfied." Table 1 indicates the distribution of responses. It is clear that faculty leaders in institutions where faculty had comprehensive or substantial roles in campuswide budgeting were more satisfied with the status quo (seven out of seven) than those whose bodies had either limited or general involvement (ten out of twenty-nine). However, these figures also make clear that comprehensive or substantial involvement was certainly not a necessary condition for faculty satisfaction with their role in budgetary affairs. Even at institutions where senate committees were involved exclusively or primarily with respect to compensation advice, three out of five faculty leaders expressed high satisfaction.

Table 1. Faculty Satisfaction with Institutional Budget Roles of Academic Governing Boards

	Level of Satisfaction			
Extent of Consultation	*Highly Satisfied*	*Mixed*	*Dissatisfied*	*Unknown*[a]
Comprehensive or substantial	7	0	0	0
Limited roles, including compensation advice	3	7	3	1
General roles	7	6	3	1
More	1	0	0	0
Totals	18	13	6	2

[a] Only administrators interviewed.

In the twelve institutions that had both faculty committees and a presence on an administrative decision-making body, faculty leaders tended to be slightly more satisfied with the administrative committees. In eleven of the twelve institutions, there was high satisfaction with the administrative body, and in one, the satisfaction was mixed. In regard to the faculty committees at these institutions, high satisfaction was expressed in eight out of twelve cases and mixed in the other four. Mixed satisfaction was expressed in the case of the one administrative body with a limited role and in four out of five cases where senate committees in these institutions had limited or general roles.

Sources of Dissatisfaction. The sources of dissatisfaction identified by leaders expressing mixed responses differed from those who were seriously dissatisfied. In several cases of mixed reaction, the major factor appeared to be that the involvement of faculty in institutional budgetary affairs was too new to have yielded positive results. One faculty leader said, "It's too early to tell; I'm hopeful. The president is committed to consultation." Another complimented the administration for trying for more openness, but viewed it as working under "constraints" that made things frustrating for both administration and faculty. This leader also acknowledged that the faculty needed to improve its handling of administrative overtures.

Where there was mixed satisfaction, complaints most often centered on making the system work, especially from the point of view of time management. One faculty leader complained, "So much needed to be accomplished in so short a time, that even if I can't say that some issues were ducked, I can say that they were worked around." Another commented that "critical allocation decisions are now being made (May), and the fiscal '92 budget proposals are needed by the Regents on June 4. It's difficult to assemble the committee right now." And still another said that "very little lead time is given for responses to some questions." Faculty leaders often recognized that their administrations wanted advice but were given unrealistic time limits by their boards.

In some institutions where such concerns were expressed, committees had felt strongly enough to make a formal complaint. Faculty leaders were hopeful, but could not guarantee that matters would improve. In several other institutions, faculty were clearly upset that the administration had tried to manage the complexities of consultation either by sometimes not consulting when it should have or by consulting only after making up its mind. One said, "All involved parties should be able to discuss matters. The administration should not produce a solution and then ask what the senate thinks. If advance consultation is encouraged enough, it will take root." Other concerns at these "mixed satisfaction" institutions involved making the process work more effectively by giving greater attention to the operating implications of capital projects, or separating longer-range planning from the domination of short-term budget concerns.

What the leaders with mixed satisfaction had in common was a belief that their institutional leaders had made a commitment to greater faculty consultation in budgetary affairs. While both administration and faculty may have been having difficulty making it work, there was hope that this could be done.

This expectation was absent among the faculty leaders who expressed serious dissatisfaction with the status quo on their campuses. In these cases, complaints centered not on matters of making the structures work, but on whether there was any willingness to create a climate for faculty involvement in institutional budgetary matters. At one of the six institutions judged to have serious dissatisfaction, the senate head implied that most committees were in abeyance. Centralized planning and other administrative activities had convinced him and his colleagues that a "proper faculty structure" was needed, but they were only now working to reactivate committees. Leaders at the other institutions where committees existed but had little influence complained bitterly. One said, "The general feeling is that many committee actions are ignored by the administration. The faculty has not a strong enough role at all levels. In no area does the faculty get beyond giving advice, which is folded in with other groups' advice." Others saw clearly that "the faculty is not part of the final decision making. . . . The committee is now shut out of the critical allocation phase, once our final funding is known" or that "the budget committee does nothing at all. Everything is done by the seat of the pants. It's ludicrous, not credible to the legislature or to anyone else. The administration does what it wants with the budget." The result was often anger and frustration, "partly because of a complex budget cycle, but mostly because the administration, although cooperative, gives only general reports and doesn't really consult."

In these institutions, the focus of discontent was less on structures than on people, and the basic commitment to consultation was in doubt. Feelings were strongest where a change of campus leadership had led to a much less collegial situation or where consultation was practiced in some areas but not in fiscal affairs. One faculty leader said, "I want to go back to who we used to have as academic vice-president. He was a former faculty leader. Then faculty leaders would have been consulted regularly." Another coupled a scathing review of current leadership with the statement, "Where you have people of goodwill working together, you have no problems." A third expressed the view that no progress would be made with respect to faculty consultation, despite good structures on paper, until the current administration moved on.

Sources of Satisfaction. As seen earlier, the extent of faculty involvement, in committees or as representative individuals on administrative bodies, was correlated with high levels of satisfaction. However, high satisfaction was also seen in about one-third of the cases where involvement was not comprehensive or substantial, indicating that there were dimensions to faculty satisfaction with their roles in budgeting other than the level of organizational involvement. Two principal additional factors emerged from the interviews. The first was the sense that the faculty bodies were able to influence the direction of the institution. The second, and perhaps the more important, was the feeling that their opinions were sought and listened to, even if there was no specific outcome that could be identified as having resulted from faculty input.

Satisfaction was clearly related to the perception that one's involvement actually made a difference. Interviewees were asked whether they felt that value had been added to the institutional budgetary process by the involvement of faculty and also whether they could identify specific examples of such influence in the past two or three years. Their perceptions of influence were related to their levels of satisfaction. Of the eighteen faculty leaders who were highly satisfied, fifteen (83.3 percent) saw their faculty committees as influential. Of the six faculty leaders who were dissatisfied, none believed that faculty committees made a difference. The thirteen faculty leaders with mixed levels of satisfaction were mixed in their assessments of influence as well. Eight of them (61.1 percent) believed that their committees were influential, while five (38.1 percent) believed that they were not.

In some cases, faculty expressed satisfaction even when their committees were not influential. In other cases, satisfied faculty who said that their committees were influential were unable to identify specific instances of such influence. What appears to account for the presence of satisfaction in the absence of felt influence, or in the presence of influence felt without examples cited, is the feeling that one "is being listened to," as expressed in comments like the following: "The administration is very open. . . . They are genuinely concerned about faculty input. They mention its desirability and utility." "People are willing to listen to what faculty have to say. Positions are respected." "The administration is very courteous and candid. . . . We don't try to second-guess it on specific allocations." "It's hard to believe there is a situation here where faculty input is not weighed." "The administration occasionally needs prodding, but generally is very open and responsive. Consultation is pretty automatic."

The sense of being listened to is what most clearly distinguished those faculty leaders who expressed any satisfaction from those who expressed none. Among the latter, faculty leaders bemoaned unwillingness to consult. Moreover, dissatisfied faculty leaders tended to ascribe their unhappiness to the personal styles of senior officers. In high-satisfaction situations, too, there was a tendency to attribute the favorable situation to personal style: "The president and provost are truly committed to consultation. I don't know how much of my positive attitude is due to the provost's commitment to consultation. Another person, within the same structure, could give us a very different outcome." "We never have the final word, but we can be very influential with the president. . . . A lot of this climate is a function of this president, who came out of the faculty and is returning to it. He came in strongly advocating faculty involvement in governance." "We have been very fortunate in our current [executive budget officer]. . . . He is even better than his predecessor. The recent ones haven't lost their faculty thinking." "The faculty are basically kept informed about what is going on and get a chance to voice concerns. . . . It's a very open situation, unlike under one former president, who—it is said—once took a vote fifteen times before he got what he wanted."

Summary and Discussion

This study of the public research universities reveals a great deal of variety in the depth of faculty involvement in budget matters and the structures through which faculty participate.

A first point concerns the absence of budgetary committees of the academic governance bodies at at least seven of the fifty-two public research universities that responded to the Gilmour survey (this volume). If to this number are added the two universities about which firm information was not available, but which gave no indication that budget or planning issues were part of their senate agendas, then 17 percent of Gilmour's public research university respondents had no organized academic focus on these resource allocation issues. While this cannot be taken to mean that there is no discussion of institutional budgetary affairs within these academic governance bodies, the absence of committees is a good indication that any such discussion is not likely to be approached systematically and that the initiative for discussion most probably rests with administrative officers. This is confirmed by the responses of these nine institutions to Gilmour. Only one response listed an actual planning or budget matter as an important past or future issue for their governance body. Three more listed "participation of faculty in planning/budget" as an important future issue, but gave no examples of planning or budget issues actually coming before their academic governing bodies.

The thirty-nine institutions contacted in this study included some whose structures for faculty participation do not offer the opportunity for extensive involvement in institutional budgetary affairs. This is clearest with respect to the five institutions whose faculty were involved solely or primarily in advice on faculty compensation. Giving advice on compensation and related policy matters can be a significant contribution to institutional governance, but when done in isolation from other areas of institutional finance is not, on its face, a budgetary function. If these five institutions are added to the nine with no apparent budget role, then at least fourteen of the fifty-two public research universities in Gilmour's study (26.9 percent) had minimal faculty involvement in budgetary affairs.

Few of the remaining thirty-eight were characterized by a wide and deep involvement of faculty in institutional budgetary matters. Thirty-four of these were contacted in the survey. Only eight had faculty on committees with comprehensive or substantial involvement, and another nine had faculty roles of varying significance but which limited participation to particular aspects of the budget. Faculty at the other seventeen institutions had a general consultative role only. If *joint effort* is taken to mean that faculty committees participate in budgeting through some structure with comprehensive authority, whether senate- or administratively appointed, then only eight institutions of the original fifty-two (15.4 percent) in Gilmour's study can be considered to have achieved that goal.

These findings can be viewed in the context of some of Gilmour's results. His respondents were asked to list the five most important issues that their governance body had addressed in the past three years and the five most important that it should address in the next three years. Gilmour's study showed that although planning, budget, and mission was the number 1 item ranked by senate heads, it was in fact a regular part of only some faculty governing bodies' agendas. Of the forty-three public research university respondents that reported having academic committees in the areas of planning and budget, only twenty-six (60.5 percent) reported that such issues were among the important ones both dealt with recently and anticipated for the future. Another eight (18.6 percent) listed no planning or budget matters among important recent or future issues. Nine (20.9 percent) cited these as future, but not past, matters for the faculty governance system, and one (2.3 percent) cited a single past issue but no future ones. Responses indicated that some of the "future" citations were based more on wishful thinking than on changes in institutional procedures.

It is of course true that faculty governance bodies could be dealing with budget and planning matters even if they are not listed among the important subjects taken up. However, the fact that 39.5 percent of the institutions that reported having faculty committees in these areas either did not list such matters as important, listed them only as future issues, or identified them as only isolated past issues raises questions about the extent of faculty involvement in central matters in which every university is engaged on a continuing basis. Certainly, this is congruent with the conclusion of the present survey that faculty involvement in institutional budgeting is not particularly deep across this group.

This somewhat negative finding about the involvement of faculty on senate or administrative advisory committees that deal with institutional budget stands in contrast to the most interesting, and in most cases recent, development revealed by the interviews: the presence of a representative of the academic governance body within an administrative budgetary decision-making structure. Such arrangements were found in thirteen of the thirty-nine institutions contacted. In eleven of the thirteen institutions, these administrative committees tended to have a comprehensive involvement in the institutional budget; in two others, the committee had a more limited role. There was no particular correspondence between the budget role of a senate committee and the presence of a senate representative on the central budget decision-making body. Of the eleven institutions, only three also had faculty governance bodies with "comprehensive" or "substantial" budgetary roles. The presence of faculty on administrative decision-making bodies does not necessarily represent a broadening of the governance body's role in budgetary affairs as much as an effort to ensure that the administrative structure has ready access to representative faculty opinion. Several of the committees of this type discovered in the present survey resembled what George Keller has called "joint big decision committees," in which "top college administrators and leading faculty are combining their efforts in a new kind of cabinet government—a novel joint policy-making committee that advises on the priorities for action, educational focus, and expenditures for the institution" (Keller, 1989, p. 137).

The presence of faculty on administrative decision-making groups was welcomed by the faculty leaders interviewed, who were by and large the ones who sat on these bodies. The significance of this development for faculty governance remains to be seen. One reason for caution is that this is a recent trend, and the mechanics have not yet been fully developed. Senates whose leaders sit on such administrative committees will need to have means for focusing on budget matters in a timely fashion and for coordinating their work with that of the individuals who represent them on the decision-making bodies. Several respondents cited problems in this area.

Both senates and administrative leaders should keep in mind what one respondent called the "heavy burden" of being the "representative" faculty member brought into administrative circles. In these cases, faculty should take particular care in whom they elect to leadership posts. Administrative officers should be mindful of this as well. If individual faculty are expected to play co-management roles, they should be given the time to do so. No one is well served by a senate leader who is asked to perform such a role as an add-on to an already overcrowded schedule.

An interesting phenomenon was the existence of more than one forum for senate discussion of budgetary matters seen at six institutions. In all but one case (which involved a senate committee with responsibility for major changes in academic units), these second groups, whether advisory to the administration or standing or ad hoc bodies appointed by the academic governing body, seemed to serve as early sounding boards for administrative officers. In several interviews, the creation of different forums for discussion was explained as due to the desire for quick, informal, and confidential budget advice to the administration. In two instances, the faculty leaders noted that the new committee seemed to be supplanting the budget role of the standing senate budget committee. It is too early to tell whether such less formally established consultative forums signal a further movement away from senate committees with institutional budgetary roles. However, several faculty leaders pointed out that their now flourishing budget committees first began as ad hoc consultative bodies during the harsh financial climate of the late 1970s, and some of the newer ad hoc bodies may develop in this direction as well.

Whatever the reasons for the establishment of these second, ad hoc committees, the maintenance of confidentiality in budget consultations seemed to be possible within the more traditional senate structures as well. Faculty leaders in three of the five institutions having senate committees with comprehensive budget involvement volunteered during their interviews that confidentiality was maintained in the committees' budget discussions and in the advice they gave to administrative officers.

Faculty satisfaction with the status quo was higher than might be expected based on the actual roles played or the influence felt by the faculty leaders. Thirty-one of the thirty-seven faculty respondents expressed either high (eighteen) or mixed (thirteen) satisfaction, with only six thoroughly dissatisfied. Those whose satisfaction was mixed were basically optimistic about changing what they did not like, while those who expressed dissatisfaction looked to the successors of the administrators they dealt with for any significant change in their present climate. The best correlates of satisfaction were (1) comprehensive or substantial involvement, (2) a sense of influence on budget outcomes, and (3) a sense that faculty opinion was sought and carefully weighed. The deeply dissatisfied faculty leaders did not appear to have any confidence that their current administrative leadership would work toward positive results in these areas.

The findings about the relationships between satisfaction and the extent of involvement, and between satisfaction and influence, indicated that faculty leaders in the public research universities surveyed expected that they and their faculty colleagues should be seriously consulted, that these expectations were met more often than not, and that the processes of consultation were at least as important as the actual budgetary outcomes. A climate of serious consultation seemed to be at least as important as the existence of mechanisms for extensive involvement in details or the existence of specific outcomes traceable to the consultation. One senate head expressed this view in saying, "The administration is open to faculty asking for input. . . . Faculty are interested not in shared governance, but in having access to decision makers and the opportunity for input. A sense of trust is very important." Similar findings about the importance of "process" benefits emerged from a recent extensive survey of institutional planning practices (Schmidtlein and Milton, 1988–1989). Analyses of university strategic planning case studies have also concluded that traditional senate structures appeared to be less useful models for faculty participation in this area than an approach that focuses on "process, on consultative decision making and the means of involving and utilizing faculty experience and expertise" (Dill and Helm, 1988, pp. 327–328).

Conclusions and Recommendations

These findings have implications not only for faculty leaders but, because of the balance of formal authority, for senior administrative officers as well. In the institutions surveyed, those who would not or could not meet faculty expectations of serious consultation were quite likely to be compared unfavorably to their predecessors or to their peers at other institutions. For the faculty leaders interviewed, who was in charge and the nature of the person's leadership style clearly mattered. Those concerned with leadership credibility in the eyes of faculty should pay attention not only to what a person has achieved but also to how the person has gone about achieving it.

There is recently renewed interest among faculty leaders in the virtues of faculty participation in university governance. Committee T (University Government) of the American Association of University Professors (AAUP) has increased its agenda in the past few years. A symposium on faculty governance now meets annually in conjunction with the American Association for Higher Education (AAHE) conference, and there is a move to develop this into a network of faculty senates for self-help purposes. Among those attending these meetings, there has not yet been extensive reporting of models of faculty participation in institutional planning and budgeting. But in the absence of data, there is concern that the 1966 "Statement on Government of Colleges and Universities" by the AAUP, Association of Governing Boards (AGB), and American Council on Education (ACE) has in some respects never reflected past practice, and there is speculation about whether it is time for a revised statement about shared governance.

The 1966 joint "Statement on Government of Colleges and Universities" is an essentially conservative document that assigns primacy in decision making to boards, faculty, and presidents, respectively, in the traditional areas of finance, academic affairs, and management. It calls for "joint effort" in a number of areas, including the allocation of resources, and interprets "joint effort" as a process of maintaining good internal communications so that all groups can have a "voice" in such matters. The statement does not particularly envisage what might be called "codetermination" of budget matters, as one might argue can be found in a few of the senates with particularly strong budget committees. It recognizes faculty membership on administrative committees as one means of maintaining communication, but likely did not envisage the extent to which this could be developed to involve a selected few faculty in central administrative decision making. In these respects, the 1966 statement is dated and vague on the mechanisms through which joint effort can be achieved. Much has happened in the quarter-century since the statement was devised. However, its overall emphasis on the need for good internal communications is still timely. The present survey indicates that institutions that do emphasize good internal communications can expect to see favorable faculty response. There is also, clearly, scope to improve in this area among the group of research universities considered in this study and, presumably, in other institutional types as well.

The 1972 AAUP "Role of the Faculty in Budgetary and Salary Matters" deals with a more limited range of topics than the 1966 joint statement and focuses on just one of the areas dealt with in the earlier statement. It emphasizes that the earlier statement stipulated "clearly understood channels of communication" and "participation by each group . . . appropriate to the particular expertise of each" (p. 170). It interprets these principles to mean that "the faculty is expected to establish faculty salary policies and, in its primary responsibility for the educational function of the institution, to participate also in broader budgetary matters primarily as these impinge on that function" (p. 170). It deals with three specific matters: problems associated with financial exigency, the role of the faculty in the determination of individual faculty salaries, and participation in budgeting. With respect to the latter, the statement takes the view that "the faculty should participate both in the preparation of the total institutional budget, and . . . in decisions relevant to the further apportioning of its specific fiscal divisions" (p. 170). Participation is viewed in terms of an "all-faculty body which may wish to formulate its recommendations independent of other groups" (p. 170). The statement does not deal with the other types of participation found in the present study—for example, faculty on administrative advisory or administrative decision-making groups—nor with the respective roles of the three basic types of groups when found in various combinations.

The present study indicates that even where participation in budgetary affairs is primarily through an all-faculty committee, involvement is usually not nearly as extensive and detailed as envisaged by the 1972 statement. In addition, the apparently increasing presence of faculty leaders on administrative decision-making committees raises a basic issue for those concerned with faculty governance. Keller (1989), for example, speculates that this kind of development may be a sign that governance, as a political activity, is giving way to an emphasis on a stronger, but more representative, management. This is not a phenomenon contemplated by the drafters of the 1972 statement, yet it is viewed with satisfaction by most of the surveyed faculty leaders who were familiar with it. This is further evidence that the existing statements of the principles of shared governance should receive careful study with a view toward a reformulation to meet the needs of institutions in the 1990s.

References

Alfred, R. L. "Organizing for Renewal Through Participative Governance." In R. M. Davis (ed.), *Leadership and Institutional Renewal*. New Directions for Higher Education, no. 49. San Francisco: Jossey-Bass, 1985.

American Association of University Professors. "The Role of the Faculty in Budgetary and Salary Matters." *AAUP Bulletin*, 1972, *58* (2), 170-172.

American Association of University Professors, Association of Governing Boards, and American Council on Education. "Statement on Government of Colleges and Universities." In American Association of University Professors, *AAUP Policy Documents and Reports, 1966 Edition*. Washington, D.C.: American Association of University Professors, 1966.

American Association of University Professors, Association of Governing Boards, and American Council on Education. "Joint Statement on Government of Colleges and Universities." In American Association of University Professors, *AAUP Policy Documents and Reports, 1984 Edition*. Washington, D.C.: American Association of University Professors, 1984.

Boyer, E. L. "Governing the Campus: A National Perspective." In J. H. Schuster, L. H. Miller, and Associates (eds.), *Governing Tomorrow's Campuses*. New York: American Council on Education/Macmillan, 1989.

Chan, S. S. "Faculty Participation in Strategic Planning: Incentives and Strategies." *Planning for Higher Education*, 1988, *16* (2), 19-30.

Dill, D., and Helm, K. P. "Faculty Participation in Strategic Policy Making." In J. C. Smart (ed.), *Higher Education: Handbook of Theory and Research*. New York: Agathon Press, 1988.

Green, J. L., Jr., and Monical, D. G. "Resource Allocation in a Decentralized Environment." In D. J. Berg and G. M. Skogley (eds.), *Making the Budget Process Work*. New Directions for Higher Education, no. 52. San Francisco: Jossey-Bass, 1985.

Guskin, A. E., and Bassis, M. A. "Leadership Style and Institutional Renewal." In R. M. Davis (ed.), *Leadership and Institutional Renewal*. New Directions for Higher Education, no. 49. San Francisco: Jossey-Bass, 1985.

Hipps, G. M. "Summary and Conclusions." In G. M. Hipps (ed.), *Effective Planned Change Strategies*. New Directions for Institutional Research, no. 33. San Francisco: Jossey-Bass, 1982.

Keller, G. "Shotgun Marriage: The Growing Connection Between Academic Management and Faculty Governance." In J. H. Schuster, L. H. Miller, and Associates (eds.), *Governing Tomorrow's Campuses*. New York: American Council on Education/Macmillan, 1989.

Lipschutz, S. S. "Leadership and the Research University." In R. M. Davis (ed.), *Leadership and Institutional Renewal*. New Directions for Higher Education, no. 49. San Francisco: Jossey-Bass, 1985.

Millett, J. D. *New Structures of Campus Power: Successes and Failures of Emerging Forms of Institutional Governance*. San Francisco: Jossey-Bass, 1978.

Mortimer, K., and Caruso, A. "The Process of Academic Governance and the Painful Choices of the 1980's." In D. G. Brown (ed.), *Leadership Roles of Chief Academic Officers*. New Directions for Higher Education, no. 47. San Francisco: Jossey-Bass, 1984.

Mortimer, K., and McConnell, T. R. *Sharing Authority Effectively: Participation, Interaction, and Discretion*. San Francisco: Jossey-Bass, 1978.

Plante, P. R. "The Role of Faculty in Campus Governance." In J. H. Schuster, L. H. Miller, and Associates (eds.), *Governing Tomorrow's Campuses*. New York: American Council on Education/Macmillan, 1989.

Pomrenke, V. "Team Leadership Development." In G. M. Hipps (ed.), *Effective Planned Change Strategies*. New Directions for Institutional Research, no. 33. San Francisco: Jossey-Bass, 1982.

Schmidtlein, F., and Milton, T. "College and University Planning: Perspectives from a Nation-Wide Survey." *Planning for Higher Education*, 1988-1989, *17* (3), 1-19.

Williams, D., Gore, W., Broches, C., and Lostoski, C. "One Faculty's Perceptions of Its Governance Role." *Journal of Higher Education*, 1987, *58* (6), 629-657.

John G. Dimond is secretary of the Governing Council of the University of Toronto.

Joint big decision committees may have the potential to improve campus management, but so far they are neither as common nor as effective as their advocates claim.

Joint Big Decision Committees and University Governance

Myrtle M. Yamada

In *Academic Strategy: The Management Revolution in American Higher Education*, George Keller (1983) contended that new forms of joint faculty-administration committees, which he labeled joint big decision committees (JBDCs), constituted the "new vortex of basic decision making on campus" (p. 4). Further, he claimed that these new bodies were "springing up like mushrooms in higher education" (p. 61) and were being forged "at a growing number of campuses" (p. 127). Keller identified six institutions at which a JBDC was said to exist, including Princeton University, Ohio University, Northwestern University, Teachers College Columbia University, Carnegie-Mellon University, and Temple University.

In 1987, I visited four of these institutions and interviewed sixty-four faculty, administrators, and students to assess the effects of the JBDC on two areas of institutional governance—academic affairs and administrative/financial affairs. I was particularly interested in examining the impact of this joint structure on the distribution of decision-making authority among the various participants (particularly the faculty), the organizational level at which decision making occurs, and the quality of campus decision making.

The Four Institutions

Princeton University established its Priorities Committee (PC) in 1969. Its responsibilities were to review the current budget, consider issues that had arisen in the course of budget preparation, and advise the president on the budget for the next academic year. It had sixteen members, including three senior administrators ex officio, six faculty, six students, and one staff member.

NEW DIRECTIONS FOR HIGHER EDUCATION, no. 75, Fall 1991 © Jossey-Bass Inc., Publishers

Northwestern University established its Budget and Resources Advisory Committee (BRAC) in 1970. Its charge was to participate with and advise the president and other senior administrators in every phase of developing both annual and long-range budgets. It had twelve members, including seven faculty and four senior administrators ex officio.

Teachers College Columbia University's College Policy Council (CPC) was created in 1972. Its role was to advise the president concerning institutional purposes and priorities and the general allocation of resources. It had forty members, including eighteen faculty, nine students, three professional staff, and ten senior administrators ex officio.

Ohio University formed its University Planning Advisory Council (UPAC) in 1977. It was to advise the provost and president on major budgetary, space, staff, and administrative issues and recommend the annual budget. It had seventeen members, including eight faculty, three members of the Dean's Council, three administrators, and three students.

Before we examine the collective experience of the four institutions with joint big decision committees, a preliminary observation is in order. Following Keller (1983), I identified JBDCs as entities meeting the following four criteria: (1) establishment in conjunction with the campus's strategic planning efforts, with a primary purpose of advising the president on the determination of campus priorities and direction; (2) functioning as a major center of campus power; (3) composed of selected faculty and administrators; and (4) secret deliberations.

The site visits and interviews revealed that two of the committees did not meet several of the criteria. In fact, only Ohio University's UPAC met all four criteria. It was the only JBDC examined that was established in conjunction with the institution's strategic planning efforts. Two of the other committees—Princeton's PC and Teachers College's CPC—were created to facilitate greater student involvement in institutional decision making. However, while the committees at Princeton, Northwestern University, and Teachers College were not specifically linked to the institution's strategic planning efforts, the reported responsibilities of the committees, particularly their budget responsibilities, met the criterion of advising the president on the determination of campus priorities and direction.

A more crucial concern was the perceived influence of Northwestern's BRAC and Teachers College's CPC. As revealed in interviews with administrators, faculty, and students at both campuses, neither body was perceived as a major center of campus influence. Consequently, only two of the four institutions visited could be regarded as having effective and influential committees that meet the criteria of joint big decision committees. The potential for the other two—BRAC and CPC—to be major centers of influence existed; both had the potential to substantially influence the development of the institution's budget, thereby affecting all the programs and operations of the institution. However, their inability to realize this potential at the time of this study cast doubt on the widespread applicability and effectiveness of joint big decision committees. Regardless of the differences between the formal definitions and the campus realities, all four institutions were included in this study.

The Impact of JBDCs on Academic Affairs

American colleges and universities have a long tradition of faculty control over academic affairs (Corson, 1975; Millett, 1978; Floyd, 1985; Baldridge, Curtis, Ecker, and Riley, 1978). There is general agreement with Mortimer and McConnell's (1982) observation that in major universities in particular, the faculties exercise effective control over the curriculum.

The institutions included in this study fall into the categories of major universities or research universities. The tradition of strong faculty control over academic affairs in these types of institutions suggests that the impact on academic affairs of any governance body not solely composed of and controlled by faculty, including any joint big decision committees, would be minimal.

The data from the four case studies support this prediction. The fifty-seven interviewees questioned about academic affairs unanimously agreed that faculty exercise strong control over academic affairs at all four institutions. At Princeton University, faculty were described as the "ultimate arbiters" of academic matters. Ohio University's curriculum was "controlled by the faculty." At Northwestern University, faculty were "paramount" in academic decisions, and at Teachers College, faculty had "complete" control over the curriculum. Faculty responsibility and control over academic affairs at the four institutions were codified in institutional statutes and regulations and faculty handbooks and verified by actual practice.

The fifty-seven interview subjects also unanimously reported that their respective JBDCs exerted minimal influence over academic affairs. The responsibilities of three of the JBDCs—Princeton's PC, Ohio University's UPAC, and Northwestern's BRAC—limited their general purview to budgetary matters. Only the CPC at Teachers College was charged with wider responsibilities, including advising the president about the purposes and priorities of the institution and reviewing proposed institutional policies relating to programs, personnel, organization, operation, and finance.

During its initial years of operation, Teachers College's CPC did influence decisions regarding academic affairs, serving as an "active legislative body" that examined numerous issues, including curriculum and instruction. Prior to the establishment of the CPC, the Faculty Executive Committee (FEC) exercised "substantial" influence over academic affairs. The Faculty Executive Committee was dissolved with the establishment of the CPC in 1972 and was gradually rebuilt in the early 1980s. The influence of the CPC on academic affairs at the time of this study was best described as nonexistent. All fourteen of the individuals interviewed at Teachers College agreed that the operation of the CPC had minimal impact on academic decision making. Financial limitations at Teachers College, however, severely constrained the faculty's control over academic issues requiring additional resources, since funding decisions were effectively controlled by administrators.

While the JBDCs at the four institutions had little direct impact on academic affairs, they influenced the academic operations of the institutions through their involvement in the budgeting process. Although the JBDCs had minimal formal input into the establishment, discontinuance, or review of academic programs, their decisions to fund, or not to fund, programs directly affected academic operations.

Both Ohio and Northwestern employed procedures to effectively limit the influence of their JBDCs over academic affairs. Ohio University preserved faculty control over academic affairs by ensuring that all funding proposals with curricular implications received prior review by appropriate faculty and university curriculum bodies before being reviewed by UPAC. Northwestern limited the influence of BRAC by restricting its budget review to general issues and broad categories.

The Impact of JBDCs on Administrative/Financial Affairs

Keller (1983, p. 61) contended that the multitude of forces facing higher education institutions required quick and vigorous institutional action. The operation of joint big decision committees, he claimed, was one response to this need: "The new committees bring together faculty, deans, and administrators; thought, numbers, and action; financial considerations, long-range plans, and programs; this year's budget, fund-raising goals, and competitive strategies. They are the policy boards in which central academic strategies are most likely to be shaped in the future (p. 175)." Further, he asserted (1982, p. 4) that these "new kinds of committees" were "increasingly active in helping to decide expenditure priorities and future emphases." The active involvement of joint big decision committees in financial and budgetary issues suggests that JBDCs would have their greatest impact on campus financial and administrative affairs.

The data in this study partially support this prediction. The major responsibility of all four bodies was to advise and participate in the review and development of the institution's annual budget. However, the actual extent of participation varied at each institution. Princeton's PC and Ohio University's UPAC exercised substantial influence over budgetary decisions. A senior administrator at Princeton reported that the recommendations of the Priorities Committee had always been adopted by the president and the trustees. Similarly, the faculty and administrators at Ohio University acknowledged that UPAC recommendations, with minor exceptions, were always accepted by the president.

The influence of PC and UPAC on budget decisions was constrained by several factors. First, both committees were limited to reviewing proposals initiated elsewhere; neither generated its own proposals. Second, PC was limited to only determining funding for general purposes and did not decide on allocations to individual schools or programs. Third, as was the case with other colleges and universities, a large percentage of each university's budget was precommitted to costs of salaries, operating expenses, and other fixed expenses. Consequently, both committees dealt only with about 1 percent of the institution's annual budget. However, PC and UPAC did effectively determine the allocation of that 1 percent.

On the other hand, the activities of BRAC at Northwestern and CPC at Teachers College were limited to reviewing the annual budget with little opportunity for participating in its development. BRAC was not viewed as a major center of influence at Northwestern. A senior administrator said that BRAC was "not a joint decision-making group" but a vehicle for "reaction and input" into budget strategies. One faculty leader acknowledged that while BRAC had "no real participation in setting the university's budget," it was seriously "listened to" by the administration, though "clearly in an advisory capacity." Only three of the twenty-one nonstudent interviewees at Northwestern believed that BRAC was influential in budget decisions. Two senior faculty members contended that BRAC had exerted a "strong impact" in shaping the budget in past years, but that its influence was declining under a new administration. A third faculty member, a former senior administrator, was the only interviewee to contend that BRAC was influential in the "central development of the budget."

The impact of Teachers College's CPC on budget decisions was unanimously acknowledged to be minimal. One faculty member described CPC as having "no teeth." A senior administrator described CPC's review of the budget as "pro forma." The review consisted of a presentation of the already prepared budget by the vice-president for finance to the CPC members followed by approximately twenty minutes of questions and answers and a vote by the committee. As another administrator commented, the budget was presented to CPC a week before it was scheduled to be presented to the trustees, so "the budget is passed because it has to be passed."

Regardless of the actual influence of these committees on the development of the institution's budget, the existence of the committees and their involvement in developing or reviewing the annual budget served to legitimize the budget process and its decisions to the university community. Princeton's PC process was described as legitimizing and bringing credibility to the budget process. The operation of Ohio's UPAC was reported to "give people confidence that the university is being run all right." A senior administrator at Northwestern thought that BRAC's involvement in budget issues "validates the credibility" of the budget process. At Teachers College, the CPC operation was cited as legitimizing the budget process.

In addition to legitimizing budget processes, how have these committees influenced the financial and administrative processes at the four institutions? The operation of these committees was credited with creating more orderly, systematic, and open processes at these institutions. According to a senior administrator, the establishment of UPAC provided Ohio University with an "orderly, systematic consultative process" that contrasted sharply with the previous highly confrontational, open budget hearings. The operation of PC at Princeton replaced the "floating group of notables" with a "formalized, continuous, more accountable" process. Even the uninfluential CPC at Teachers College was credited with creating a more open, public budget process. A senior long-time faculty member contended that "the budget-making process is because of the CPC a very, very public matter. Prior to the existence of the CPC . . . the faculty and the community in general were hardly advised at all about what was happening." According to a senior faculty member at Northwestern, BRAC was established to try to bring "rationality" to the budget process. Under the present administration, BRAC processes were described as "formalized, open, and organized."

Finally, the operation of these committees was credited with creating more representative budget processes. Prior to the establishment of these committees, budget decisions were generally made by senior administrators with input from selected faculty members—for example, Princeton's "floating notables." The establishment of the four committees provided for formal participation by other members of the university community. At Northwestern, faculty were formally included in the budget process, while Princeton, Ohio University, and Teachers College included faculty, students, and professional staff.

A Redistribution of Influence

The establishment of the four committees had virtually no effect on the governance processes concerning academic affairs at the institutions studied, and only minimal effect on actual decisions regarding academic/curricular issues except as those issues required additional resources or funding approval. The impact of these committees on financial/administrative decisions varied from substantial at Ohio and Princeton to minimal at Northwestern and Teachers College.

The establishment of the committees was credited with creating more systematic, formalized, and open budget processes. Additionally, the committees provided for formal representation by faculty and other constituencies in these processes. How did the establishment of the Priorities Committee, the University Planning Advisory Council, the Budget and Resources

Advisory Committee, and the College Policy Council affect the distribution of decision-making authority among the various participants in these financial decisions? Specifically, how was the role and decision-making authority of the faculty altered?

Jencks and Riesman (1968) reported that faculty in modern American universities by the late 1960s asserted more authority than they had in earlier times. By 1982, however, conditions in American higher education had changed so significantly that Mortimer and McConnell (1982, p. 161) warned that faculty authority might "suffer erosion" under the pressure of greater budgetary control, increased demands for accountability, and periods of financial stress. Faculty involvement in financial decision making has never been high (Dykes, 1968; Garbarino, 1975; Floyd, 1985; Baldridge, Curtis, Ecker, and Riley, 1973), and Baldridge (1982) warned that financial difficulties facing American higher education were pushing budget-making authority gradually upward, out of the reach of the faculty. Keller (1982, p. 4) argued that as a result of faculty reluctance to decide budget cuts, "power is shifting from the faculty to the campus leaders." He suggested that "the choice has passed to administrators to make the new, hard decisions. Leadership has shifted, and with it power. . . . After six decades of increasing faculty control and power, and after especially forceful faculty power from the mid 1950s to mid 1970s, the presidents, provosts, and deans are becoming strong again."

Keller maintained that because of this shift in power, higher education governance was "groping for new forms" and that "new kinds of joint faculty-administration committees are increasingly active in helping to decide expenditure priorities and future emphases."

Keller's enthusiasm for these "new forms" was not necessarily shared by other commentators. Powers and Powers (1984, p. 49) contended that joint big decision committees could "pose a serious threat to collegial governance" and cause "further atrophy and even death of faculty senates or school-level governing bodies." Floyd (1985, p. 37) also cautioned that "overall, joint big decision committees could hinder . . . the development of a decision-making culture that provides for the broad involvement of faculty."

These warnings suggested that the establishment of JBDCs might tend to shift governance from a broader-based participation to one of administrative dominance and thus diminish faculty influence in decision making. It might also tend to shift faculty participation in governance from traditional groups such as senates to less representative modes of participation. What actually happened at the four institutions?

Faculty Influence. The experience of the four institutions with their committees varied considerably. The operation of Princeton's PC and Ohio's UPAC significantly increased faculty influence in financial affairs. The thirteen individuals interviewed at Princeton unanimously agreed that the operation of PC had increased faculty influence. The establishment of PC replaced decision making by "floating notables" with a formal mechanism for faculty input into budget decisions. Faculty members made up the largest constituent group within PC and were acknowledged to exert significant influence over committee deliberations and decisions.

The establishment of UPAC also provided a formal mechanism for faculty participation in financial affairs at Ohio University. Eleven of the twelve interviewees questioned about changes in faculty influence agreed that the operation of UPAC had substantially increased faculty influence. A senior administrator claimed that the faculty involvement in UPAC "strengthened the credibility of faculty participation in governance" throughout the institution. In addition to generally increasing faculty influence in financial affairs, the inclusion of the five members of the Faculty Senate Executive Committee on the council also increased the influence of the faculty senate in financial affairs.

While the members of PC and UPAC were actively involved in preparing and reviewing their institution's budgets, the budget purview of Northwestern's BRAC and Teachers College's CPC was limited to reviewing a budget that had been prepared by senior administrators. BRAC functioned strictly as an advisory body to Northwestern's president rather than as a decision-making body. As described earlier, the impact of BRAC on financial decisions at Northwestern was marginal. However, the establishment of the committee provided the first formal mechanism for faculty input into budgetary decisions. Consequently, while the committee did not make specific funding decisions, the operation of the committee increased faculty input into budget decisions.

Teachers College's experience with CPC provided the only substantial support for the idea that a JBDC could reduce faculty influence. The operation of CPC resulted in severely diminishing the faculty's role in governance, initially causing the dissolution of the Faculty Executive Committee, the body that had served as Teachers College's faculty senate. The CPC's impact on faculty influence was described as having "diluted the faculty voice in governance," leading to the "disempowerment of the faculty." Faculty were described as being "disenfranchised."

Administrative Influence. Did the increase in faculty influence over financial affairs at Princeton, Ohio, and to a lesser extent Northwestern diminish the administrative role in decision making? The data from these institutions show that the administrative role continued to be strong. Interviewees at both Princeton and Ohio described the administrative role in the budget as one of "guiding" or "leading" the process. At both institutions, the senior administrators were the only long-term continuing committee members. They were consequently more experienced than most of the committee members and were responsible for educating the new members about the budget process. A PC member at Princeton commented, "Administrators lead the procedures. They raise and answer many of the questions partially because they are more experienced and knowledgeable. They try to direct the discussions and have an idea of where the budget should go but are never overbearing about it." A faculty member commented that while the PC process took longer to reach decisions and complicated the work of administrators, the presence of more constituencies actually strengthened the administrative role, as the administrators were responsible for reconciling the views of the various constituencies.

Administrators at both Princeton and Ohio exercised substantial influence over budget decisions by establishing the guidelines and preparing and analyzing budget projections and other financial data used by the committees. Administrators at Ohio University were described as guiding the UPAC process with a "firm hand" using information and persuasion. In addition, senior administrators contributed significantly by performing preliminary analyses of the budget and the various funding proposals submitted to the committees.

While faculty input into budget decisions increased with the operation of BRAC at Northwestern, the president was acknowledged to "hold the upper hand" in decision making. Indeed, because BRAC's role was limited to providing reaction and input to the budget, which was prepared by the president and senior administrators, administrators exercised significant control over financial decisions.

These data support the contention that influence and power in higher education institutions are not zero-sum games. In examining perceived changes in power in sixty-eight universities between 1964 and 1971, Gross and Grambsch (1977, pp. 35–36) found "a general tendency to believe that the power of most of the power holders had risen," suggesting a situation in which a wider spectrum of participants were able to influence each other to a greater extent than previously.

The establishment of joint big decision committees at the four institutions did not shift governance from a broader-based participation to one of administrative dominance. In fact, with the exception of Teachers College, governance shifted from administrative dominance to broader-based participation and a corresponding increase in faculty influence, albeit with strong administrative guidance of the processes.

Faculty Governance Bodies. While the establishment of CPC was responsible for the initial demise of the Faculty Executive Committee at Teachers College, the committees at Ohio and Northwestern did not negatively affect the faculty senate organizations at those institutions (Princeton has no organized faculty senate). The faculty members of BRAC were all appointed by the General Faculty Committee (GFC), Northwestern's faculty senate organization. Three of the members are members of GFC.

Similarly, five of the eight faculty members of UPAC at Ohio University constitute the membership of the Faculty Senate Executive Committee.

While UPAC's budget responsibilities were credited with weakening the role of the senate's finance committee, the inclusion of the executive committee on UPAC was acknowledged to have generally increased the influence of the faculty senate in financial matters.

The established faculty governance organizations at the four institutions, including Princeton's standing faculty committees, were primarily concerned with the review and determination of academic matters. As reported previously, the four committees had only minimal influence over academic matters through their power to determine funding levels for various academic programs and proposals. Consequently, the operation of the committees had minimal impact on those institutions' faculty governance organizations.

Locus of Decision Making

Baldridge (1982, p. 14) argued that in response to budget crises, "a substantial shift toward centralized authority" has occurred in higher education institutions: "More and more decisions are being moved higher into the administrative hierarchy and farther away from the point of action. Decisions that were once made in departments are now made by deans; decisions that were once made by deans are now moved up to the vice-presidential and presidential level." Keller (1982, p. 4) agreed, claiming that "presidential leadership is back" and maintaining that power has shifted from faculty to campus leaders. He identified this shift in power as one of the features of the management revolution occurring in American higher education. The establishment of joint big decision committees was another feature of that revolution. Consequently, it might be expected that the operation of a JBDC would reflect this centralization of authority and shift the locus of decision making to higher organizational levels.

Such a shift did not occur at any of the four campuses, and no increased centralization was noted. With respect to academic affairs, the actual locus of decision making at the institutions remained with the faculty and the various faculty committees and organizations. Additionally, financial decisions at Northwestern and Teachers College continued to be made at the senior administrative level. However, financial decisions at the two institutions that operated influential joint big decision committees— Princeton and Ohio University—were altered to be effectively determined by PC and UPAC. Although these committees served to *advise* the president on the formulation of the institution's annual budget, the recommendations of the committees were consistently accepted by the presidents. Consequently, instead of shifting the locus of decision making to higher organizational levels, the formation of a JBDC meant that budget decisions were determined at slightly lower organizational levels at Princeton and Ohio University.

Quality of Decision Making

Joint big decision committees, according to Keller (1983, p. 127), are established to "insure prompt deliberations and give wise advice on important matters." Certainly, a major motivating factor in establishing these committees was the desire to improve the quality of campus decision making in the face of changing conditions and challenges. The operation of joint big decision committees should increase the participation of various groups in decision-making processes, an outcome that is widely believed to improve the quality of academic decisions. Goheen (1969, p. 7), for example, noted that "as long as faculty and students are inclined to effective participation, it is in everyone's best interest, I believe, to draw on what they can contribute. For when decisions are discussed widely and hammered out jointly among the principal parties of interest, they tend to be sounder institutional decisions." The operation of joint big decision committees might therefore be expected to enhance the quality of campus decision making.

The operation of three of the committees—all except CPC at Teachers College—were strongly perceived to have improved the quality of decision making. Eleven of thirteen individuals at Princeton agreed that the operation of PC had significantly enhanced quality; eight of nine individuals at Ohio University believed that quality had improved; and nine of thirteen individuals at Northwestern reported a positive impact on quality. Decisions were described as more informed, more thoughtful, and better prepared. Further, a faculty member at Ohio University contended that proposals received a "fairer hearing" in the UPAC process and were less dependent on personalities. A senior administrator at Northwestern suggested that BRAC's major role was that of quality control over budget decisions, and he believed that decisions were both substantively and politically better owing to the formal provision for faculty input into the process.

The operation of CPC, perceived to have had a minimal impact on academic and budget decisions at Teachers College, was viewed by the fourteen interviewees as having no impact on the quality of decision making at the institution.

Conclusion

The establishment and operation of the four JBDCs did not alter governance procedures regarding academic affairs at the institutions. Faculty control over academic affairs within departments and established faculty committees and senate organizations continued to be strong.

The operation of the Priorities Committee at Princeton and the University Planning Advisory Council at Ohio University shifted governance regarding financial affairs from administrative dominance to broader-based participation. Faculty influence over financial decisions at these two institutions increased significantly. While strong administrative dominance of financial matters continued at Northwestern University, the operation of the Budget and Resources Advisory Committee resulted in greater faculty input into these decisions. The tradition of administrative dominance over financial matters at Teachers College remained unchanged by the operation of the College Policy Council.

While the initial demise of the Faculty Executive Committee at Teachers College supports concerns that the establishment of joint big decision committees could cause the atrophy and death of faculty senates, the experience at the other three campuses does not. In fact, the influence of Ohio University's faculty senate was judged to have increased with the operation of UPAC. In addition, the operation of CPC at Teachers College did not prevent the reestablishment of the Faculty Executive Committee. In sum, the impact of the establishment of the four committees on existing faculty governance bodies was either positive or neutral.

The impact of the committees on the locus of decision making at the four institutions varied. The operation of the committees resulted in lowering the organizational level at which financial decisions were effectively determined at two institutions. At the other two institutions, no changes were experienced.

At three of the four institutions (excepting Teachers College), the operation of the committees was judged to have enhanced the quality of decision making. At two of the institutions, quality was perceived to have improved significantly; at the third, the committee exercised "quality control" over financial decisions. At the fourth institution, the committee was viewed as having had no impact on quality.

Benefits Resulting from JBDCs. As reported earlier, only two of the four committees examined—Princeton's PC and Ohio's UPAC—were perceived to be major centers of campus influence and can thus be considered, strictly speaking, joint big decision committees. These two committees were judged to have broadened participation, increased faculty influence, enhanced quality, and lowered the organizational level at which financial decisions are determined. The operation of these committees positively affected the institutions in several additional ways.

First, each of the two committees contributed to improved morale. The operation of PC and UPAC provided formal mechanisms for participation in the decision-making processes of the institutions. The perceived influence of these committees resulted in a widespread belief that meaningful opportunities for participation in campus decision making existed at Princeton and Ohio University. This sense of participation is crucial to faculty morale and satisfaction. The Carnegie Foundation for the Advancement of Teaching (1986, p. 33) reported that "participation in institutional decision making is the most important factor in faculty satisfaction at doctorate-granting and comprehensive institutions." Anderson (1986) found that meaningful participation of faculty in governance had more effect on faculty morale than the level of institutional financial support and faculty salaries. Bowen and Schuster (1986, p. 22) reported that "an important feature of faculty participation in the making of institutional policies and decisions is that it has a strong influence on faculty morale. Faculty members are intelligent and highly educated people who feel qualified to have opinions not only on matters affecting them personally and their departments, but also on matters pertaining to the institution as a whole. They also feel entitled to know about events and forces and decisions that are affecting the institutions. Therefore reasonable involvement of faculty and communication with them are critical in the decision-making process of any college or university."

The experiences at Princeton and Ohio support these findings. Morale at Ohio University since the establishment of the University Planning Advisory Council was reported as significantly improved. While UPAC operations cannot be credited with sole or major responsibility for this improvement, a senior administrator maintained that the UPAC process "substantially reduced the tension and anxiety level" on campus. He credited the UPAC process with creating a "feeling of goodwill and good faith on the campus." The high morale observed at Princeton University was a result of a multitude of factors rooted in Princeton's history, culture, and people. The operation of the Priorities Committee with its opportunity for serious participation in budget decisions was only one factor that reinforced the positive attitudes that all interviewees evidenced toward the institution. These experiences dispute Powers and Powers's (1984, p. 49) caution that joint big decision committees "might tend to depress campus morale because the average citizen could feel manipulated instead of in control of his or her own destiny."

Second, participation in joint big decision processes at Princeton and Ohio University was credited with creating a more informed university community. A major role of both PC and UPAC was informational. Both committees were described as "educating the community" on the general motivations and processes for the allocation of resources. A faculty member at Ohio University claimed that this informational role served to both inform the faculty about the condition of the university and inform the administration about faculty concerns.

A third consequence of the operation of the joint big decision committees was their positive impact on the relationship between faculty and the administration. The operation of PC and UPAC were judged to have fostered good relationships between faculty and administrators. Twelve of fourteen individuals questioned at Ohio described the relationship as "better than it's ever been" and cited UPAC's operation as helping to foster and maintain these good relations.

Princeton is credited with having a long tradition of good relationships between faculty and administrators. Five of nine interviewees at Princeton maintained that the operation of the Priorities Committee fostered these positive faculty-administration relations. The remaining four interviewees believed that PC had no impact on a pre-existing and continuing positive relationship.

The less influential Budget and Resources Advisory Committee was also credited with improving faculty-administration relationships at Northwestern. The existence and operation of the committee was judged to have prevented major confrontations by providing administrators with an "early warning system." The operation of the committee was also viewed as a sign that administrators were willing to listen to faculty input and thus helped to ease tensions between the two groups.

Fourth, the operation of joint big decision committees improved communication within the university community. Even when the committees were not viewed as major centers of influence, they were acknowledged as important vehicles of communication. At Northwestern, BRAC was described as a "major center of communication" and the "best communication link" between faculty and administration. All twenty-one faculty members and administrators interviewed at Northwestern concurred that providing a communication link between the faculty and the administration was an important function of the committee. A senior administrator at Teachers College judged the College Policy Council to be "useful" because it facilitated communication across the various groups in the college. These comments refute another concern of Powers and Powers (1984, p. 49) that joint big decision committees "might hinder rather than help information flow."

Essential Factors. The experiences at Princeton and Ohio University, and to a lesser extent at Northwestern, reveal the potential for joint big decision committees to improve governance in colleges and universities. Joint big decision committees have the potential to (1) increase participation in campus decision making, (2) increase faculty influence in campus decision making, and (3) enhance the quality of campus decision making. Further, joint big decision committees can positively impact campus morale and faculty-administration relationships, create a more informed university community, and serve as important centers of communication. To realize this potential, it is crucial that these committees be accorded significant decision-making powers. Recommendations of these committees must, with only minor exceptions, be accepted by senior administrators. A senior administrator at Ohio University feared the possibility that the administration might at some time be unable to accept the recommendations of UPAC. He acknowledged that should this happen, the credibility of the system would be fatally damaged.

Moreover, it is essential that these committees make actual decisions and not just react to prepared budgets. At Princeton, the Priorities Committee determined actual funding levels for various activities and acted on proposals for funding of new programs or additional funding of existing programs. At Ohio University, the University Planning Advisory Council determined the distribution of a planning pool fund amounting to approximately 1 percent of the total budget. To realize their potential, these committees must be able to make decisions and have these decisions generally accepted by the president.

Skillful leadership, committed to the process, is also essential. A senior administrator at Princeton University contended that "intelligent, wise, thoughtful leadership" was crucial. To better ensure the "acceptability" of committee decisions, administrators need to provide realistic guidelines and set parameters for committee deliberations and decisions. Administrators must also provide committee members with accurate and adequate information. This administrative involvement ensures that informed decisions will result from committee deliberations.

Committee membership is crucial. As administrators and faculty members at Princeton said, committee members must be "serious, intelligent, competent, responsible, respected" members of the university community. One method of ensuring that committees are made up of quality members is for the provost or president to appoint a significant portion of the membership, with input from appropriate organizations. This way, committee membership can reflect a balanced representation of subject areas, special competencies, length of tenure, and experience. All members of Princeton's PC were appointed by the provost with input from the various departments and organizations. The membership of UPAC at Ohio University reflected a balance between members elected by their constituencies and those appointed by the provost. On the other hand, none of the members of BRAC or CPC were appointed by senior administrators. A senior administrator at Northwestern recalled a "series" of "bad" BRAC members who "kept energy focused on wrong issues." The inability of the president or provost to ensure that BRAC and CPC membership included faculty whom they considered competent, quality participants is probably one factor in the limited role these committees played in budget preparation and review.

The Future of JBDCs

George Keller has contended that a new kind of committee is spreading across the landscape of academic institutions. However, reports by Keller and others on joint big decision committees have revealed only six institutions—Princeton, Ohio University, Northwestern University, Teachers College, Carnegie-Mellon University, and Temple University—as having established these committees. While the purpose of this study was not to ascertain the prevalence of these committees, the limited number of identified joint big decision committees casts doubt on Keller's claim that they are "springing up like mushrooms." Additionally, conversations with Keller in 1987 did not yield the names of additional institutions whose JBDCs might have been established more recently.

Carnegie-Mellon, identified by Keller as having a joint big decision committee, was not visited in this study. Temple University was identified by Keller in two publications (1982, 1983) as operating a joint big decision committee. However, according to senior administrators and staff at Temple University, through conversations and correspondence in 1987, Temple's Resource and Priorities Committee (identified by Keller as Temple's JBDC) has never functioned as a joint big decision committee. In addition, neither the Budget and Resources Advisory Committee nor the College Policy Council were judged by interviewees at Northwestern and Teachers College to be joint *decision-making* committees, as neither body was viewed as a "major center of campus influence." Consequently, of the six committees identified by Keller, three were clearly not true joint big decision committees.

Finally, Keller implies that these joint big decision committees are a relatively new phenomenon. However, of the four institutions studied, only Ohio's UPAC could be considered a "new" body, having been established in 1977. The other committees were established in 1969, 1970, and 1972. Although the concept of the JBDC has been linked to the process of strategic planning, in fact the primary motivation for their formation was not to improve planning, but to improve governance.

These findings do not negate the potential for joint big decision committees to improve campus governance. Their limited numbers, however, do cast doubt on their ability to become a major force in campus governance and management in the years ahead.

References

Anderson, R. E. *Finance and Effectiveness: A Study of College Environments.* Princeton, N.J.: Educational Testing Service, 1986.

Baldridge, J. V. "Shared Governance: A Fable About the Lost Magic Kingdom." *Academe,* 1982, *68,* 12–15.

Baldridge, J. V., Curtis, D. V., Ecker, G. P., and Riley, G. L. "The Impact of Institutional Size and Complexity on Faculty Autonomy." *Journal of Higher Education,* 1973, *44,* 532–547.

Baldridge, J. V., Curtis, D. V., Ecker, G. P., and Riley, G. L. *Policy Making and Effective Leadership: A National Study of Academic Management.* San Francisco: Jossey-Bass, 1978.

Bowen, H. R., and Schuster, J. H. *American Professors: A National Resource Imperiled.* New York: Oxford University Press, 1986.

Carnegie Foundation for the Advancement of Teaching. "The Satisfied Faculty." *Change,* 1986, *18,* 31–34.

Corson, J. J. *The Governance of Colleges and Universities: Modernizing Structure and Processes.* (Rev. ed.) New York: McGraw-Hill, 1975.

Dykes, A. R. *Faculty Participation in Academic Decision Making.* Washington, D.C.: American Council on Education, 1968.

Floyd, C. E. *Faculty Participation in Decision Making: Necessity or Luxury?* ASHE-ERIC Higher Education Report No. 8. Washington, D.C.: Association for the Study of Higher Education, 1985.

Garbarino, J. W. *Faculty Bargaining: Change and Conflict.* New York: McGraw-Hill, 1975.

Goheen, R. F. *The Human Nature of a University.* Princeton, N.J.: Princeton University Press, 1969.

Gross, E., and Grambsch, P. V. "Power Structures in Universities and Colleges." In G. L Riley and J. V. Baldridge (eds.), *Governing Academic Organizations: New Problems, New Perspectives.* Berkeley, Calif.: McCutchan, 1977.

Jencks, C., and Riesman, D. *The Academic Revolution.* Chicago: University of Chicago Press, 1968.

Keller, G. "The New Management Revolution in Higher Education." *AAHE Bulletin,* 1982, *35,* 3-5.

Keller, G. *Academic Strategy: The Management Revolution in American Higher Education.* Baltimore, Md.: Johns Hopkins University Press, 1983.

Millett, J. D. *New Structures of Campus Power: Successes and Failures of Emerging Forms of Institutional Governance.* San Francisco: Jossey-Bass, 1978.

Mortimer, K. P., and McConnell, T. R. *Sharing Authority Effectively: Participation, Interaction, and Discretion.* San Francisco: Jossey-Bass, 1978.

Powers, D. R., and Powers, M. E. "How to Orchestrate Participatory Strategic Planning Without Sacrificing Momentum." *Educational Record,* 1984, *49,* 48-52.

Myrtle M. Yamada is associate director, Curriculum Research and Development Group, College of Education, University of Hawaii, Manoa.

INDEX

Academic affairs, JBDC impact on, 81-82
Academic senates. *See* Senate(s), academic
Adler, D. L., 28, 38, 39, 61
Administration: and governance system, 46-48; influence of, 86-87. *See also* Leadership
Administrative/financial affairs, JBDC impact on, 82-84. *See also* Budgeting
Alfred, R. L., 64, 77
American Association for Higher Education (AAHE), 7, 11, 23, 25, 27, 41, 43, 61, 75
American Association of University Professors (AAUP), 63, 76, 77; Committee T, 27-28, 38, 39, 75
American Council on Education (ACE), 63, 75, 77
Anderson, R. E., 90, 94
Association of Governing Boards (AGB), 63, 75, 77

Baldridge, J. V., 7, 8, 13, 15, 19, 23, 24, 27, 28, 38, 39, 45, 61, 81, 85, 88, 94
Bassis, M. A., 64, 77
Begin, J. P., 8, 23
Ben-David, J., 8, 23
Berdahl, R. O., 16, 23, 28, 39
Birnbaum, R., 2, 3, 5, 6, 7, 25, 37, 42, 43, 45, 59
Blau, P. M., 8, 18, 23
Boismier, J., 5
Bowen, H. R., 58, 61, 91, 94
Boyer, E. L., 2, 5, 64, 77
Broches, C., 64, 78
Budgeting, faculty role in, 3-4, 63-76. *See also* Administrative/financial affairs
Bureaucracy, university as, 10-11
Burnett, J. H., 19, 23

Cameron, K. S., 43, 61
Carnegie Commission on Higher Education, 8, 23
Carnegie Foundation for the Advancement of Teaching, 2, 5, 8, 10, 23, 41, 61, 90, 94

Carnegie-Mellon University, 79, 93, 94
Caruso, A., 64, 77
Cater, D., 18
Chaffee, E. E., 45, 61
Chan, S. S., 64, 77
Cohen, M. D., 13, 15, 17, 21, 23
Collective bargaining, 38; study results on, 32-33
Collegium, university as, 10, 11
Columbia University. *See* Teachers College Columbia University
Committee(s): executive, 30-31, 44; standing, 31
Corson, J. J., 13, 23, 81, 94
Council, as governance body name, 30
Cox, R. S., 5
Curtis, D. V., 13, 15, 19, 23, 38, 39, 81, 85, 94

Deegan, W. L., 17, 23
Deutsch, M., 13, 23
Dill, D., 27, 39, 64, 75, 77
Dimond, J. G., 3, 4, 63, 78
Duff, J., 16, 23
Dykes, A. R., 13, 18, 23, 85, 94

Ecker, G., 13, 15, 19, 23, 38, 39, 81, 85, 94
Edelstein, S., 28, 39
Etzioni, A., 14, 23
Executive committee, 30, 31; role of, 44

Faculty: attitude of, toward governance, 41; budgeting role of, 3-4, 63-76; as governance body name, 30; influence of, 85-86; and JBDC, 4; opinion of, of senates, 8; participation of, in policy making, 38; quality of, and governance system, 45-46
Fairweather, J., 5
Feldman, M. S., 12, 23
Floyd, C. E., 8, 24, 81, 85, 95

Garbarino, J. W., 85, 95
Gilmour, J. E., Jr., 3, 4, 27, 39, 43, 44, 46, 48, 61, 64, 65, 71, 72
Goheen, R. F., 89, 95

Gore, W., 64, 78
Governance, 42–43; future actions on, 4–5; interest in, 1–2
Governance bodies, participative, 27–28, 38–39; chairs of, 32, 35; and collective bargaining, 32–33; executive committee of, 30–31; important issues of, 34, 36; organization, operations, and support of, 29–30; perceptions of, 33–34; standing committees of, 31; strengthening of, 36, 37; study of, 28–29, 37–38. *See also* Governance systems; Senate(s), academic
Governance systems: and administration, 46–48; cultural issues of, 45–46; improving effectiveness of, 58–60; and leadership, 57–58; and research, 60–61; of Rural State College, 54–56; of Southern State College, 51–53; structural issues of, 43–45; of Urban Community College, 48–50. *See also* Governance bodies, participative; Senate(s), academic

Grambsch, P. V., 87, 95
Green, J. L., Jr., 64, 77
Gross, E., 87, 95
Gunne, M. G., 41, 62
Guskin, A. E., 64, 77

Helm, K. P., 64, 75, 77
Hipps, G. M., 64, 77
Hobbs, W. C., 9, 10, 11, 24
Hodgkinson, H. L., 7, 13, 24

Ikenberry, S. O., 27
Institutional Leadership Project, 42

Javitz, H., 5
Jencks, C., 85, 95
Joint Big Decision committees (JBDCs), 4, 79, 89–90; and academic affairs, 81–82; and administrative/financial affairs, 82–84; benefits from, 90–92; and decision making, 88–89; essential factors with, 92–93; at four institutions, 79–81; future of, 93–94; and influence redistribution, 84–88
Joint effort, 63, 64, 72, 75

Keller, G., 4, 5, 8, 10, 11, 18, 19, 24, 43, 61, 73, 76, 77, 79, 80, 82, 85, 88, 89, 93–94

Kemerer, F. R., 7, 8, 23, 24, 27, 28, 38, 39, 45, 61
Kerr, C., 19, 24

Ladd, E. C., Jr., 14, 17, 24, 41, 61
Leaders, formal, 14
Leadership: continuity of, 46; development of, 59–60; and governance, 56–57; and senates, 57–58
Lee, B. A., 3, 5, 41, 45, 46, 61, 62
Leslie, D. W., 41, 62
Lieberman, M., 9, 13, 24
Lipschutz, S. S., 64, 77
Lipset, S. M., 14, 17, 24, 41, 61
Lostoski, C., 64, 78

McConnell, T. R., 8, 11, 13, 17, 24, 27, 38, 39, 64, 77, 81, 85, 95
Magarrell, J., 18, 24
March, J. G., 12, 13, 15, 17, 21, 23
Masland, A. T., 19, 24, 45, 61
Mason, H. L., 8, 16, 24
Merton, R. K., 9, 14, 22, 24
Millett, J. D., 8, 10, 11, 13, 24, 27, 39, 42, 43, 62, 64, 77, 81, 95
Milton, T., 74, 78
Monical, D. G., 64, 77
Mortimer, K. P., 8, 11, 13, 17, 23, 24, 27, 38, 39, 41, 62, 64, 77, 81, 85, 95

National Center for Postsecondary Governance and Finance, 42, 64
Northwestern University, Budget and Resources Advisory Committee (BRAC) at, 79, 80, 89–94; and academic affairs, 81–82; and administrative/financial affairs, 82–84; and decision making, 88–89; and influence redistribution, 84–88

Ohio University, University Planning Advisory Council (UPAC) at, 79, 80, 89–94; and academic affairs, 81–82; and administrative/financial affairs, 82–84; and decision making, 88–89; and influence redistribution, 84–88
Olsen, J. P., 15, 23
Organized anarchy model, of senate, 20–23

Personnel, screening device for, 17
Plante, P. R., 64, 77

Political system, university as, 10, 11
Pomrenke, V., 64, 78
Powers, D. R., 85, 95
Powers, M. E., 85, 95
Princeton University, Priorities Committee (PC) at, 79-80, 89-94; and academic affairs, 81-82; and administrative/financial affairs, 82-84; and decision making, 88-89; and influence redistribution, 84-88

Research: need for, 38-39; role of, 60-61
Riesman, D., 85, 95
Riley, G. L., 13, 15, 19, 23, 38, 39, 81, 85, 94
Ritual, senate as, 19
"Role of the Faculty in Budgetary and Salary Matters," 76
Rural State College (RSC), 54-56
Russell, S. H., 1, 5

Scapegoat, senate as, 19-20
Schmidtlein, F., 74, 78
Schuster, J. H., 58, 61, 91, 94
Senate, as governance body name, 30
Senate(s), academic, 7-9; criticism of, 3; effectiveness of, 3, 4; functions of, 9-20; organized anarchy model of, 20-23; survey of, 3; in symbolic organizational systems, 20-23. *See also* Governance bodies, participative; Governance systems
Smircich, L., 21, 24

Southern State College (SSC), 51-53
Standing committees, 31
Stanford Project on Academic Governance, 27, 37, 38
"Statement on Government of Colleges and Universities," 75-76
Status, senate as provider of, 13-15
Stone, J. N., Jr., 11, 24
Symbol, senate as, 12-13

Teachers College Columbia University, College Policy Council (CPC) of, 79, 80, 89-94; and academic affairs, 81-82; and administrative/financial affairs, 82-84; and decision making, 88-89; and influence redistribution, 84-88
Temple University, 79, 93, 94
Tierney, W. G., 10, 24, 45, 61
Trow, M., 18, 24

University, models of, 10-11
Urban Community College (UCC), 48-50

Veblen, T., 2, 5, 8, 24

Weick, K. E., 20, 21, 22, 24
Wildavsky, A., 16, 24
Williams, D., 64, 78
Williamson, C., 5

Yamada, M. M., 4, 79, 95

Zimbler, L. J., 5

ORDERING INFORMATION

NEW DIRECTIONS FOR HIGHER EDUCATION is a series of paperback books that provides timely information and authoritative advice about major issues and administrative problems confronting every institution. Books in the series are published quarterly in Fall, Winter, Spring, and Summer and are available for purchase by subscription as well as by single copy.

SUBSCRIPTIONS for 1991 cost $45.00 for individuals (a savings of 20 percent over single-copy prices) and $60.00 for institutions, agencies, and libraries. Please do not send institutional checks for personal subscriptions. Standing orders are accepted.

SINGLE COPIES cost $13.95 when payment accompanies order. (California, New Jersey, New York, and Washington, D.C., residents please include appropriate sales tax.) Billed orders will be charged postage and handling.

DISCOUNTS FOR QUANTITY ORDERS are available. Please write to the address below for information.

ALL ORDERS must include either the name of an individual or an official purchase order number. Please submit your order as follows:
Subscriptions: specify series and year subscription is to begin
Single copies: include individual title code (such as HE1)

MAIL ALL ORDERS TO:
Jossey-Bass Inc., Publishers
350 Sansome Street
San Francisco, California 94104

FOR SALES OUTSIDE OF THE UNITED STATES CONTACT:
Maxwell Macmillan International Publishing Group
866 Third Avenue
New York, New York 10022

OTHER TITLES AVAILABLE IN THE
NEW DIRECTIONS FOR HIGHER EDUCATION SERIES
Martin Kramer, Editor-in-Chief

HE74   The Changing Dimensions of Student Aid, *Jamie P. Merisotis*
HE73   Using Consultants Successfully, *Jon F. Wergin*
HE72   Administrative Careers and the Marketplace, *Kathryn M. Moore,
       Susan B. Twombly*
HE71   Managing Change in Higher Education, *Douglas W. Steeples*
HE70   An Agenda for the New Decade, *Larry W. Jones, Franz Nowotny*
HE69   Financial Planning Under Economic Uncertainty, *Richard E. Anderson,
       Joel W. Meyerson*
HE67   Achieving Assessment Goals Using Evaluation Techniques, *Peter J. Gray*
HE66   Improving Undergraduate Education in Large Universities, *Carol H. Pazandak*
HE65   The End of Mandatory Retirement: Effects on Higher Education,
       Karen C. Holden, W. Lee Hansen
HE64   Successful Strategic Planning: Case Studies, *Douglas W. Steeples*
HE63   Research Administration and Technology Transfer, *James T. Kenny*
HE62   Making Computers Work for Administrators, *Kenneth C. Green,
       Steven W. Gilbert*
HE61   Leaders on Leadership: The College Presidency, *James L. Fisher,
       Martha W. Tack*
HE60   Increasing Retention: Academic and Student Affairs Administrators in
       Partnership, *Martha McGinty Stodt, William M. Klepper*
HE59   Student Outcomes Assessment: What Institutions Stand to Gain,
       Diane F. Halpern
HE58   Financing Higher Education: Strategies After Tax Reform, *Richard E. Anderson,
       Joel W. Meyerson*
HE57   Creating Career Programs in a Liberal Arts Context, *Mary Ann F. Rehnke*
HE56   Managing Programs for Learning Outside the Classroom, *Patricia Senn Breivik*
HE55   Crisis Management in Higher Education, *Hal Hoverland, Pat McInturff,
       C. E. Tapie Rohm, Jr.*
HE53   Managing College Enrollments, *Don Hossler*
HE52   Making the Budget Process Work, *David J. Berg, Gerald M. Skogley*
HE51   Incentive for Faculty Vitality, *Roger G. Baldwin*
HE45   Women in Higher Education Administration, *Adrian Tinsley, Cynthia Secor,
       Sheila Kaplan*